Interp
Comm
Innovi
Instru

Copyright © 1978
National Education Association of the United States

Stock No. 1497-9-00 (paper)
           1496-0-00 (cloth)

Note:
The opinions expressed in this publication should not be construed as representing the policy or position of the National Education Association. Materials published as part of the NEA *Aspects of Learning Series* are intended to be discussion documents for teachers who are concerned with specialized interests of the profession.

Library of Congress Cataloging in Publication Data

Friedman, Paul G
    Interpersonal communication.

    (Aspects of learning)
    Bibliography: p.
    1. Interpersonal communication. I. Title.
II. Series.
BF637•C45F74   301.14   78-582
ISBN 0-8106-1496-0
ISBN 0-8106-1497-9 pbk.

To my son Jeremy — may he grow up in
an environment of open, caring communication.

The Author

Dr. Paul G. Friedman is Associate Professor of Speech Communication and Human Relations at the University of Kansas, Lawrence.

The Consultants

The following educators have reviewed the manuscript and provided helpful comments and suggestions: Jeff Golub, teacher of Language Arts and Speech, Kent Junior High School, Kent, Washington; Jamie K. Mehl, English teacher, Shawnee Mission West High School, Shawnee Mission, Kansas; and Dr. Elaine Yarbrough, Assistant Professor, Department of Communication, University of Colorado, Boulder.

Contents

PART ONE

New Directions in Communication Education

The classes in communication that I currently teach bear little resemblance to those I attended twenty years ago. Most, in fact, would startle my old instructors, if viewed from their orientation at that time. Even the terms used in the titles, "interpersonal," "human relations," etc., weren't part of the vocabulary we used then when discussing our field.

I feel pleased as I consider these changes, for two reasons. First, I have always sought, as a personal propensity, to work at the creative edge of my profession. I must admit that there is a rebellious streak in me which restlessly strives to reach beyond traditional limits in many things that I do. But I believe, too, that this aspect of my nature is well suited to the discipline in which I have chosen to work. It seems to me that one branch of communication education must inherently be somewhat "countercultural."

A teacher in this field can view himself or herself, at any given time, in one of two ways. On the one hand, he or she may be helping people who are dysfunctional, who have difficulty in communication, who need to adapt to or better integrate themselves into the mainstream of social interaction. The teacher helps them to fit in more unobtrusively. This work is remedial. Its function is to assist those students to learn how most people think, feel, and act and then how to operate in order to become a congenial, accepted member of most social groups. Much basic course work in interpersonal communication and programs dealing with speech anxiety pursue this end. Conformity, comfort, adaptation are their underlying goals.

On the other hand, when one assumes that students are already minimally competent in social interaction, a second level of operation rises to the foreground. In secondary schools and colleges today a large proportion of students are preparing themselves for careers in professions wherein mature ability to deal with people is a primary skill. Personnel administration, education, and helping professions of all sorts attract the "people-oriented" segment of the student population. This group already recognizes a special interest, or even a talent, for human relations within themselves, and they want to capitalize upon it in their future professional work.

To stress basic skills of interaction or fundamental confidence-building with them would be superfluous. They already possess these competencies. Their need is to be challenged beyond the limits of common, everyday patterns of interaction, to work with dimensions usually avoided in normal discourse, to fill out the repertoire of skills and situations which they can handle. Directions and approaches for this level of work need to be sought outside traditional channels and settings, in places where social rebels and artists live, in "outlaw" territory, in the counterculture.

This leads me to the second reason for feeling good about the new directions in teaching that I have taken. The society in which I live has experienced many changes in the past two decades. What once were small, isolated, avant-garde phenomena soon became widespread social movements which now impact on everyone's daily life. Consequently, the new wave is quickly absorbed or co-opted into the mainstream, and the fresh becomes the familiar. Once they become common, everyday occurrences, social forces must be accounted for in educational curricula—especially those in communication, the medium through which people from disparate environments must exchange their perspectives on life.

I would like to describe briefly some of the social changes I have witnessed in the last 20 years that have most influenced our field and, more particularly, my own thinking. Not all are accounted for in the material in this volume. But their influence permeates my personal and professional views, and thus are worth sharing. These phenomena may be seen, as well, as seeds from which further new directions in communication might still emerge. They are not presented in any particular order; their significance depends on the particular context in which an instance of instruction occurs.

A. *The emergence of minorities.* When I think of people who will most certainly be mentioned when the history of our times is written, Martin

Luther King quickly comes to mind. The civil rights movement that he and others pressed forward, especially during the 1960's, opened up many new opportunities for members of racial minorities. Previously, people in positions of power, as well as those in oppressed groups, had mainly to deal only with others of similar background. As integration progressed, new attention had to be given to the communication customs governing simple, everyday events which are handled quite differently among people from subcultural groups who ordinarily live out their lives without direct contact with each other.

B. *Consumer advocacy.* Ralph Nader, I believe, is another individual who has had a profound influence on our times. His efforts opened the gates for consumers to question and vocally challenge the quality of the goods and services they receive from both private and public institutions. There is now greater sensitivity than ever before on the part of officials who deal with the public regarding the handling of complaints, the disclosure of the inner workings of complex systems, the ethical standards employed in making decisions, etc. We might credit, as well, "Deep Throat," the mysterious informant who broke open the Watergate scandal, for focusing popular attention on the credibility of public officials. Now, we view more critically the manner in which candidates for public trust present themselves. This applies at the grass roots as well as at the national level, when they interact informally as well as when they speak from an official platform.

C. *The women's movement.* The opening up of new opportunities for women to assume positions of authority has directed attention to some neglected dimensions of interpersonal communication, especially to the exploration of processes whereby controversial points of view can be expressed firmly, yet without traditionally "unfeminine" aggressiveness. Under the heading of "assertiveness training," we now have a more subtle sense of how to articulate conflicts in a manner that is least likely to arouse defensiveness, while permitting a frank exchange of ideas.

D. *The instability of marriage.* Nontraditional roles for women also play a role in the rising divorce rate. For many other reasons as well, the ties that traditionally bound husband and wife together for a lifetime have been loosened, thereby allowing "incompatibility" to be a common, acceptable reason for divorce. The hardships accompanying such a split motivate new efforts toward understanding how differences can be negotiated and how alienated couples can be reconciled. In large part, such efforts involve educating marriage partners in the communication skills needed to discuss their feelings, to resolve conflicts, and to provide mutual support.

E. *The generation gap.* Within families there must be communication between parents and children. Within social institutions, such as the church, the school, and the military, people in authority usually are a generation older than those whose efforts and commitment they must win and guide. Rapid changes in social norms have made their task increasingly difficult. Young people no longer as readily identify with and model themselves after their elders. College students I teach report that they find their younger siblings in high school responding differently to common crises, such as

11

dealing with drugs, sex, job, etc., than they did. Consequently, parents and professionals who work with youth are relearning "parenting" and "helping" skills that render their communication efforts more capable of overcoming the misunderstandings that arise when people of different ages must live and work together.

F. *Mobility.* More than ever, people move from place to place in the course of their lives. The college population has risen dramatically, creating larger numbers of highly educated individuals who "can't go home again," who must relocate to obtain employment in their field of expertise. Such a move requires the quick establishment of work and social relationships not based on years of growing familiarity and intimacy. As a result, the need increases for skills necessary to share oneself and to reach out to others as a conscious, deliberate step in interaction. Initiating and deepening relationships rapidly has become a communication demand of our times.

G. *Affluence and beyond.* As the American economy grows and more people realize their fundamental dream of having a house, a car, and other amenities, the human energy used to gain these ends can then be turned in new directions. Not surprisingly, material possessions do not necessarily bring complete fulfillment. The striving for more gratification often is rechanneled toward developing richer personal relationships. People want to enjoy the fruits of their labors with others whom they care about, who care about them, and with whom they can share their inner struggles. To develop relationships at deeper levels of intimacy requires more sensitive communication abilities than are needed for talking over everyday material life tasks.

H. *Self-determined destinies.* As life experiences become more enriched and complex, as work and social opportunities become more diverse and less restricted by one's inherited social status and locale, more flexibility for individualized life-styles emerges. People feel free to select from a variety of work arrangements, family alternatives, and social groups. Choices, options, decisions are continual. Dialogue about "Who am I?" "What's best for me?" "Where do I go from here?" is increasing. Processes for personal decision-making, such as values clarification, self-awareness, life-planning etc., abound, and these involve specific communication skills.

I. *Popularization of psychology.* Earlier in this century, the techniques used by professionals in helping professions were couched in jargon unintelligible to laymen. A psychiatrist was a mysterious shaman with categories of diagnosis and treatment expressed in multisyllabic terms. Recently, however, these have been translated by popular writers into everyday terms such as "parent, adult, child," "top dog—underdog," and "I'm okay, you're okay." Books offering such direct, manageable terms have hit the best-seller lists and given tacit permission for people to discuss their innermost concerns with one another, rather than deferring immediately to a professional counselor.

J. *Support groups.* One helpful dimension of communication in a time of stress is the provision of "empathy" or putting oneself in the other's shoes as a means of allowing that person to feel fully understood. What more direct route to this end exists than sharing one's predicament with others who need not imagine the experience but who actually have been there themselves. Alcoholics Anonymous provides this kind of support, as do innumerable other mutual help groups that have proliferated in the last two decades. Examples are groups for overweight people, gamblers, smokers, women seeking greater liberation, parents of handicapped children, homophiles, single parents, and many others. Such support groups emphasize particular approaches to communication heretofore common to only the closest of friends.

K. *Breakdown of inhibitions.* The last two decades have seen a growing diminishment of social taboos in the wider discussion of issues raised in such support groups. People who are homosexual feel freer to reveal their orientation publicly. Couples initiate talk about their sexual needs and preferences openly, relying less on innuendo and subtle hints. Most recently, the feelings accompanying the imminence of death have become better understood and more acceptable. As these intense life moments are increasingly available to open dialogue, communication sensitivity becomes even more essential.

L. *Growth centers.* New movements in communication education rarely arise in classrooms of major universities. They require experimental growth and nurturance in a more protected atmosphere. The "greenhouse" for many recent innovations has been the growth center. At bucolic retreats, such as the NTL center in Bethel, Maine, and Esalen Institute in Big Sur, California, workshops offered in secluded, protected, supportive environments have extended the limits of expression as well as the methods for exchanging messages among participants. The group work, exercises, and especially the fundamental permissiveness experienced at such "off-the-beaten-path" centers have profoundly expanded the limits of instruction within the "establishment."

M. *Organic orientation.* At growth-center workshops, participants have released, expressed, catharted extraordinarily deep levels of formerly inhibited emotions. Quite consistently these releases were followed by powerful feelings of good will, warmth, and intimacy among those involved. This outcome supported the notion that, fundamentally, human beings have a healthy inner core which is encrusted by defenses created to deal with harsh treatment. Such assumptions lead to approaches to communication education that stress a caring, supportive atmosphere that allows one's "natural," real self to emerge. The process of instruction becomes one of gently peeling off layers of inhibition and defense, rather than only programming in new instructions for students to follow.

N. *Mind-body integration.* Another awareness that has emerged over the last few years is a fuller sense of how an individual's body reflects his or her state of mind and vice versa. Communication anxiety, for example, is an emotional state with pronounced physiological symptoms. Since such stress generally is unpleasant and dysfunctional, reducing it is part of an instructor's goals. This end may be approached by altering one's cognitive views of the situation, by encouraging emotional expression of the feeling, or by suggesting physical relaxation exercises. Each method addresses one facet of a systemic condition of stress. Thus, instructors, now more than ever, look at the human beings they teach in a holistic way and examine the biology, as well as the psychology, of communication.

O. *States of consciousness.* In considering how the mind works, we have added another level for examining human behavior. It is now understood that the left and right hemispheres of the brain perform distinct functions— the former tuning in to more logical, linear phenomena, the latter to more intuitive, holistic perceptions. In addition, we know that the mind can experience several states of consciousness each of which yields a different posture vis-a-vis other people. As we learn more about how to consciously control these states of mind and the effects each has on human interaction, we will have significant new tools to use for enriching communication education.

P. *New exchanges.* In recent years there have been some extremely fertile exchanges between communication education and other disciplines. The open classroom movement in education has provided a model for individualizing instruction that is well suited to this field, wherein there exist many alternative modes of learning, each best suited to a particular kind of learner or learning goal. The "social skills training" movement in clinical psychology has highlighted the role of interaction competence in mental health and has provided means for diagnosing and treating problems in this area. The interest in "creative problem-solving" in the field of business has generated several group techniques which must be applied through skillful use of oral communication. The "poor or open theatre" techniques of Jerzy Grotowski and Joseph Chaikin suggest an exercise-filled training program that serves to enlarge the capacity for emotional and physical self-expression of actors in ways that expand upon techniques employed in communication workshops. The methodologies for personal growth being imported from the Far East, such as meditation, yoga, and the martial arts, have provided alternative, traditional approaches for achieving the calm, centered, integrated state of being from which the communicator is most effective.

This last list of "borrowed" concepts could go on and on. We are in a bountiful, stimulating period in the history of our profession. Many kernels of knowledge can be mixed in a communication curriculum to increase its nutrient value. The task of an educator in this field today, I strongly believe, is to maintain an open mind and an open syllabus so that both can accommodate fresh input. The task of discerning and integrating worthwhile elements into our classroom, of applying our existing concepts and techniques to new social contexts, and of developing instructional methodologies to carry out these processes most effectively is an exciting, challenging one. I hope this volume is perceived as making a small contribution toward the execution of this task.

PART TWO

Reframing Paradigms

Note

My intention is to propose innovative approaches to communication education. I hope to be creative, to map out heretofore unexplored territories in which to carry out our work. In doing so, one can take several perspectives. One can describe new routes for reaching commonly agreed upon destinations. One can suggest new techniques for bringing everyone along those routes more quickly and enjoyably than is traditional. Or, one can fly above the entire terrain and point out how various routes and means for traversing them (which seem unrelated) are similar or significantly different and, thus, may be seen in a new configuration. The last approach is the purpose of the upcoming section.

A field of study progresses by taking a "giant" step every so often, followed by a series of "baby" steps (to use terms I recall from a childhood game) that are smaller moves within the scope of the initial leap forward. This happened about a decade ago when interpersonal communication was introduced and then gained an established place in the communication course catalog. Since then, a plethora of textbooks has been published aimed at covering this new territory. Each has some small contribution to make in adding to or refining that material. I assess the length of stride each takes by perusing its contents. Once, when the territory was largely uncharted, I was excited about reading this material from cover to cover. Recently, I find myself most often skimming volumes as they arrive and nodding with familiarity at the chapter titles and subsections that review material in ways I have seen many times before.

These common ways of organizing or "framing" our discipline have demonstrable value, otherwise they wouldn't be as popular as they are. Nevertheless, they also have their limits, as does any system for drawing distinctions among interrelated areas. A growing field needs to review familiar paradigms for organizing ideas and to consider whether alternative approaches might better suit its needs.

One reason familiar frames of reference prevail is that we develop means for implementing them which are commonly used. It is relatively easy to propose a new paradigm, but that suggestion must be accompanied by practical classroom experiences for it to be truly useful. This criterion is adhered to in the subsequent chapters. Each presents an overview of how communication education (in the interpersonal domain) can be viewed and then proposes several means for carrying out that vision in daily classroom exercises.

CHAPTER 1

Hard and Soft:
The Foundations of
Communication Education

I

I recently served briefly as a consultant to a large corporation. The ostensible problem was a lack of productivity among typists in the word-processing division. Interviews revealed a number of hypothesized causes. These ranged from a time-and-motion oriented personnel manager's measures of the microseconds required to move fingers across a typewriter keyboard to the grumblings of middle managers about autocratic, un-responsive administrators. Each explanation had validity and was poten-tially useful.

The situation was reminiscent of the parable about the six blind men whose descriptions of an elephant were based on the parts of the animal each had touched. Likewise, curricula and text material in our field reflect the points at which we touch the amorphous entity called communication. We each hope to improve students' functioning in this activity by stressing development of awareness and skills of different dimensions. Some address minute particles of behavior such as articulation or kinesics; others consider broader variables such as persuasion or intimacy. If we draw an analogy between perception of an organization's functioning and that of an individual, the former is equivalent to looking at the specific steps taken by an employee on the job, the latter at the decisions of the president.

Someone concerned with measurement of change is likely to examine the employee's (or student's) output. Indeed, that is an obvious test of individual effectiveness. Inside the organization, however, people often attribute their success or failure to the direction or treatment they receive from superiors. Harry Truman's desk plaque, "The buck stops here," attests to this propensity.

The use of behavioral objectives in education directs attention to the specific responses of the learner. These are the "gidgets" we are trying to

17

produce. Nevertheless, phenomenologically, these responses emerge from instructions transmitted by a higher control center. Because this administrative function in an individual is not available to observation, it is sometimes ignored. Yet the power of the "black box" makes it an attractive target for influence. Deeper changes promise many surface manifestations.

One way to approach an understanding of such central processes is to synthesize the ways in which they are expressed in observable behaviors and to identify common denominators. By examining many instructional procedures which seem to pursue overlapping outcomes, we might infer some basic properties which would encompass all, and some fundamental processes which all are trying to affect. Thus, we can discuss and employ these procedures more parsimoniously.

The field of communication education currently is being stretched and extended to incorporate more aspects of human interaction than ever before. Once its domain covered public, polite, somewhat formal contexts only. Now, more private, personal events of raw, everyday life are being considered. Target behaviors include self-disclosure, expressing empathy, being assertive, etc. We can consider all of the new and the more traditional practices as unique and thereby justify the proliferation of units of study. On the other hand, however, we can see each as a clue or a symptom of overarching, central processes that govern large areas of human communication.

Any movement to proliferation can become dangerously diffuse. Energies can be scattered and thus rendered ineffectual. Consequently, efforts at integration must accompany forays into new areas. It can be helpful to label the forest, as well as the trees. The purpose of this chapter is to propose a frame of reference with which to trace back to their roots, circumscribe, and define the foundations of the many manifestations of communication education.

II

An examination of the lists of best-selling nonfiction in the last couple of years reveals two major thrusts among people's interests. One is toward means for greater relaxation, sensual pleasure, peace of mind, and self-acceptance.[1] The other is toward greater control, power, and influence.[2] These two tracks correspond well with discoveries of how the human body and mind function.

Physiologically, there seem to be two extremes of systemic operation. At one end is a "fight-or-flight" response. When we perceive ourselves to be under threat of attack, as is likely in the complex, changing, demanding conditions of modern life, our organisms undergo "an involuntary response that includes an increase in blood pressure, heart rate, rate of breathing, blood flow to the muscles, and metabolism, preparing us for conflict or escape."[3] These reactions are triggered by activation of the sympathetic nervous system (which results in secretion primarily of the hormone epinephrine).

The other extreme has been termed the "relaxation" response. When an individual feels calm, receptive and safe, the earlier mentioned conditions are reversed. Blood pressure, heart rate, breathing, blood flow to the muscles, and metabolism are all slowed down. The flow of epinephrine is minimized.

Concurrent with these somatic states are specific brain functions. There seems to be a comparable division of labor between the right and left hemispheres of the brain.[4] When one is trying to force change on the environment, or believes a situation must be actively controlled, as when stress or conflict exists, the left hemisphere is dominant. It is the control center for linear, logical, analytic, calculating mental functions. When one is more at ease, feels safe and receptive, the right hemisphere is the locus of activity; it perceives more holistically, intuitively, creatively, spatially.

There is also a corresponding difference in the speed of brain wave activity. The frequency of brain waves increases when one is planning, worrying, feeling agitated. Brain waves are slower when an individual is relaxed, experiencing pleasure, peace of mind, or an absence of threat.[5]

In sum, a human being seems to oscillate between two poles of experience. These modern scientific findings were previewed in the Taoist philosophy of Lao-tzu, who postulated the forces of *yin* and *yang*, passive and active energies in man. These are not mutually exclusive dualities. They are "like the different, but inseparable, sides of a coin, the poles of a magnet, or pulse and interval in any vibration. There is never the ultimate possibility that either one will win over the other, for they are more like lovers wrestling than enemies fighting."[6]

Ancient and modern observers of these attributes of being agree that the optimally effective individual is one whose inner state and outer response can be controlled in a manner appropriate to the conditions which must be dealt with. The danger to be avoided is being stuck at one extreme or the other—responding from either posture in a consistently conditioned, rigid way to the flux of circumstances encountered in life—when the alternate or a mixture would be more appropriate.

It is my contention that most contemporary approaches to communication education can be seen as methods to help one make such adaptations in his or her organism and in his or her means for encoding and decoding messages. These two systemic conditions or mind-body states are the foundations of communication education.

III

The constructs fight-flight and relaxation, left and right brain dominance, yang and yin are all ways of describing the ends of the continuum on which one can view instructional methodologies. However, I choose to employ related terms which seem to suit my purposes better. I prefer to encapsulate each syndrome of conditions under the headings *hard* and *soft*. Each is composed of a constellation of factors that seem to co-exist when each of these states predominates.

19

It has been my observation that in a given moment an individual is doing one of two things: either trying to change the environment or trying to understand and deal with it as it is. In other words, he or she seeks to have an impact, to be an active force, to be *hard*; or he or she is being open to receive, to learn, to be *soft*. Neither exists in a pure state. One is usually dominant and the other less present, ready to take its turn when the inner and outer forces of the situation shift. At rare moments, they do exist in a tenuous state of balance, and this is a point at which the individual is performing optimally.

An illustration which epitomizes these states to me is drawn from the oriental martial arts. Some, such as karate, are said to be hard forms. Picture the warrior who can direct energy through a hand with such concentration and force that a thick board of wood can be split in half. One whose hand or leg or body is so strong and controlled that he or she can, through this laser-like, concentrated force, have an irresistible impact on virtually any obstacle is indeed a powerful individual. Mind and body coordinate to emit a hard, compact energy stream. Such a person can intimidate, persuade, overpower anyone in this way. Hence, this person is fearless.

Other systems of martial arts, such as *t'ai-chi-ch'uan* or *aikido* are called *soft* forms. In these, the practitioner achieves power by being completely aware of forces in the environment and by being flexible enough to step aside at the approach of such forces so that they fall over from inertia. This is the method of "not forcing" or "going with the grain, rolling with the punch, swimming with the current, trimming sails to the wind, taking the tide at its flood, and stooping to conquer . . . an opponent is defeated by the force of his own attack, and the latter art reaches such heights of skill that an attacker is thrown to the floor without even being touched."[7] This individual never becomes tense or rigid; he or she need never clash; he or she knows what is going on around him or her; he or she understands the need and direction; he or she cannot be struck; hence he or she is fearless.

These same states of being can be applied to one's stance when communicating with people. Embedded within virtually every approach to personal growth in the realm of communication is a method for willfully maximizing one or the other of these states, for helping students to be harder or softer. A useful synthesis of many approaches emerges from applying this concept to each.

IV

We are particularly concerned in communication education with optimizing students' powers in relationships, with developing their abilities to achieve their goals and to avoid being overwhelmed or manipulated by others. We have said that someone who can be hard or soft at will has taken a step in this direction. Now we must define the specific properties of the hard and soft ends of the continuum as they apply to human interaction.

We have said that neither posture ever exists purely, exclusive of the other. For the purpose of explanation, however, it is helpful to portray each as an extreme, as a virtually homogenous set of conditions. In doing so, one can recognize characteristics of individuals as they appear at moments of social intercourse. Nevertheless, this description is intended to exaggerate differences, not to mirror reality.

A *hard* system emerges from a state of dissatisfaction, a sense of desiring or even demanding that something in the environment change, a position of being in a struggle with others, as when someone drives a *hard bargain* or when one has *hard feelings*. That person is seen as aggressive or as seeking to achieve something, a *hard worker*. Such action clearly is directed, aimed, purposeful, as is evident in a *hard sell*. Such a person is concerned with an effect on others, with changing their behavior, with getting more. Attention is focused on the surface of things, on their external, obvious side—as when someone wants only *hard data*, *hard facts*, or *hard cash*. Toward this end the individual values moving along, doing things, being active; he or she is attuned not to what he or she is, but to what he or she can become. Such action is concentrated, focused. This person is attentive to the goal, as when one stares or takes a *hard look* at something. The aim is to be precise, accurate, correct, controlled in one's efforts. There usually is appreciation for an approach that is ordered, planned, formed or structured. The superstructure of computers, called the *hardware*, fits this description. Something ordered this way operates logically, scientifically, in a *hard-headed* mode. It can be seen as a mechanical, synthetic way of being. It proceeds by analyzing, distinguishing among the parts of things; it implies a limited pathway; it clearly demarks what is necessary and what isn't, what belongs and what doesn't; thus, a hard force is efficient, economical, parsimonious, spare, not wasteful. These are the conditions mandated by a *hardship*, being *hard up*, or when there is *hardly enough* to do the job. Such a state requires being selective, discriminating, restrictive, or critical, as in being *hard to please*. To be so, one often must be tough, unrelenting, stubborn, or even rigid. Phrases such as *hard and fast*, *hard-nosed*, etc., express this attitude. Such a person knows what he or she wants and what he or she wishes to avoid; he or she is likely to project these values onto others, being prescriptive, even judgmental.

A person required to be hard must often protect himself or herself to the point of being insensitive, and is seen as *hard-shelled* or *hard core*, invulnerable or unavailable. At the extreme this person can become cold, harsh, even cruel, as in *hardhearted*, meting out what seems to be *hard treatment*. Nevertheless, the form emerges as compact, solid, tight, like a *hard knot*, and the impact is intense, strong, forceful, powerful. The phrase *hard liquor* depicts the kick a hard system has, or we can return to our first image of a *hard-fisted* chop that splits its target into pieces.

On the other hand, a *soft* mind-body system usually exists when an individual is content with things as they are. One accepts, even appreciates what one perceives. Consequently, one is in a receptive state, willing to take in what is coming, or in a generous state, willing to give away possessions or to serve others. Someone like this is seen as *a soft touch*. He or she is warm, kind, soothing, a *soft-hearted* person, readily loving and understanding, empathic. Such a person can see deeply into things and is concerned with

21

essential causes, spirituality, inner feelings, and the quality (rather than the quantity) of objects. In other words, he or she can perceive many levels operating simultaneously; he or she is fascinated more by the internal domain than by surfaces. One tends to be still and quiet at these times, aware of what is happening at present, just being rather than anticipating the future. The pace is likely to be leisurely, slow. Attention and behavior are fluid, shifting readily, intuitively, from thing to thing. There is a diffuseness, a spaciousness to one's view of phenomena. Movement and growth are welcomed. One sees holistic, unifying connections among apparently different things. Natural, organic forms are preferred. One is inclusive, absorbing, allowing of apparently inappropriate combinations. One is as permissive of impulses inside oneself, as in others; the tendency is to be spontaneous, impromptu, flowing, free. One expresses oneself openly, and so is often viewed as intuitive, emotional, even sentimental, *a softy*. The tendency is to be lenient, tolerant of others, welcoming their free self-expression, to be flexible in response. One values depictions or descriptions of things as they are, rather than efforts to control, manipulate, or change them. One allows oneself to be affected by others, one cares, responds fully, and thus is *soft-skinned*, vulnerable, delicate. The mode of dealing with contentious situations is to be very aware, passive, mild, nonviolent; to sidestep the blows until the storm has blown over, dissipated itself.

V

Each state of being clearly is of greater value in some situations than others. Too often, individuals advocate one or the other as more natural, more realistic, more virtuous, more effective, etc. Whether viewed from the perspective of utility, morality, or human nature, both postures, or mixtures thereof, are essential to healthy, successful human functioning. What must be known is *when* it is best to be mostly hard or soft, and *how* to carry out the desired transition.

Certain conditions in one's environment, including the posture of the person(s) with whom one is dealing, seem to call for one or the other to be dominant. This section will describe the circumstances in which first hardness and then softness would be most appropriate.

The body-mind state of hardness, and its relevant communication skills, is appropriate when the people discoursing are primarily responsible for creating a product, realizing a goal, or otherwise have a tangible end that must be attained. A work foreman, a teacher, or anyone who values what is to be accomplished by oneself and co-workers or subordinates must be able to be hard at times. When obstacles must be overcome or when endurance is needed, during the course of a multistage project, a hard, focused, forceful approach is desirable. This is especially true whenever the method for reaching the goal is obvious or when discussion of the means is completed and a choice has been made. Whenever a plan of action is apparent and ready to be implemented, a hard approach is appropriate. When time is a factor, in cases where there is a need to act quickly, to rush in order to meet a deadline, to take advantage of a momentary opportunity, to make a snap decision, or to avoid wasting time, a hard approach to relating is best. Similarly, when resources are scarce or limited, or when one is involved in a competitive situation, a hard style is called for. If uncertainty is a danger and a show of strength or confidence is needed, or if obedience and adherence to rigid role expectations are valued, then a leader (e.g., a military officer) is wise to communicate from a hard posture. If a simple exchange of information is desired, or a sweeping surface-level question must be answered, as in a lecture or when taking a survey, a hard, direct approach can do the job. Additionally, when the fundamental, basic skills of a discipline are to be learned, a hard, parsimonious procedure often is used.

On the other hand, when enjoyment or satisfaction are high priorities in a situation, a soft approach is desired. When no overt action is necessary, or before a choice is made when appropriate action is not yet clear, and alternatives and their consequences need to be considered, then softness is valued. If there are ample time and resources for whatever dialogue or task is to be accomplished and the future seems secure, a soft stance is appropriate. This is true, as well, if unavoidable setbacks occur, or if a situation is unchangeable and must simply be endured. To feel and express emotions, especially tenderness, caring, love, to develop commitment, encourage individual investment and initiative, to collaborate closely in an intimate relationship, whether personal or professional, a soft mode of relating is desirable. Finally, when seeking to know someone or to learn about something deeply, at many levels, or when developing excellence or creativity in an art, a soft approach works best.

These conditions can vary from moment to moment in any situation. Individuals who are successful in human relations can detect shifting circumstances and adapt accordingly, or they can consciously create the change themselves. For example, when we set or extend the amount of time allowed for a committee meeting, we are anticipating the kind of interaction that will take place. A short meeting with concrete objectives tends to promote hard communication. A leisurely meeting with no pressure to make decisions or produce results will encourage soft communication. Most meetings begin with soft interaction and evolve into hard exchanges, as time and patience evaporate. After the meeting ends soft interaction prevails once again.

At times consciously and at times unconsciously, members and leaders sense and adapt to these shifts. Someone who does not, who is hard when soft conditions prevail, is seen as inappropriately aggressive. Someone who is soft when hard interaction is required is seen as wishy-washy, long-winded, time-wasting.

Just as external social circumstances naturally call for an alternation between hard and soft responses, so, too, within an individual's short and long-range life cycles, there is a need for waves of each kind of response. We know that a person's health is jeopardized if one does not take some time each day to soften up, to relax and appreciate the moment, instead of being active or anxious. There also are times when an individual feels that his or her energies are too scattered, that he or she lacks discipline and sense of direction, that he or she needs to be harder. There seem to be innate desires within people both to achieve, to forge ahead, to be hard; as well as to love, to be intimate, to be soft. When either of these desires is not being naturally fulfilled, as a matter of course, then a need arises for special training. Most often we flow from hard to soft to hard, etc., without conscious effort. When this cycle is broken, when an individual feels trapped in one-half of it, like a needle stuck in one groove of a record, repeating the same mind-body state until it is annoying, then it would be of benefit to be able to call upon a method for shifting gears.

VI

A contention of this chapter is that most instruction in communication is intended at its foundation to effect a transformation from a soft to a hard approach to relating, or vice versa. Speaking in broad generalities, courses in rhetorical communication hope to empower students to be harder and courses in human relations or interpersonal communication try to develop softer qualities. Course titles, however, are applied to a wide range of classroom experiences not necessarily consistent with the dichotomy being postulated here.

More specifically, for a course to develop hardness certain processes must be stressed. Whenever one is moving toward identifying or clarifying values, goals, or priorities, one is preparing for harder communication. When we know what we want, when we define an objective, and when we turn our attention toward achieving this end to the exclusion of others, we are focusing on being hard. By eliminating distractions, low priority issues, opposing points of view, etc., one's attention and energies can become concentrated. This is what occurs when an orator identifies a precise goal for a speech, a salesperson imagines the customer placing an order, a debater works on one side of a case, an individual selects a career line after talking with a vocational counselor, or whenever someone makes a decision.

After a direction is set, a plan of action or a means for implementing the decision and attaining the goal is developed. Once this is done, the individual is fully launched upon a hard mode of relating. This is the instruction we provide on how to organize, develop and deliver a speech, how to be assertive, how to give useful feedback, or most other "how to's" in the repertoire of communication education. These plans add the dimension of focus, compactness, and hardness to one's presentation of self.

When someone is hard, feeling driven, anxious, impatient, yet the situation seems more appropriate for soft behavior and/or inwardly he or she is yearning to relax, be calm, more peaceful, then another set of techniques would be called for. Muscular relaxation can begin this shift. There are several ways by which one can voluntarily reduce the degree of tension in one's body, thereby shifting from the fight-flight preparedness of the hard state to the relaxation response of the soft state. Moving into a quiet, peaceful environment, where one isn't surrounded by unfinished tasks that hook the hard side, can also be helpful. Keeping one's awareness in the present moment instead of contemplating future outcomes helps to create a soft state. Being available to messing around, trial and error, nonjudgmental actions, responding to intuitive impulses, etc., are all ways of letting go to a soft state. A loss of self-consciousness, absorption in phenomena outside oneself, sensory contact with another person, seeking to understand or experience rather than to evaluate or manipulate—all are aspects of softening.

It would be beneficial to include a unit of study in hardness and softness at the beginning of a course on communication. Students would not only be asked to understand the characteristics of these two states of being; they would develop greater awareness of the overt signs of these states in order to perceive them in others. They would also learn how to shift at will from one to the other themselves. Experiences using the senses of sight, hearing, and touch to accomplish specified tasks and then simply allowing each sense to wander freely for enjoyment's sake only, provide a basic awareness of the difference. When students sense their ability to shift from soft to hard, and back again voluntarily, they realize how they can control these shifts as the need arises. Next, they can be asked to walk, draw, write, and perform a variety of other simple tasks—first, with the intent of accomplishing something; then, spontaneously without conscious aim, just playing with each task, to experience each fully at the moment it occurs. Thus, they broaden their ability to control each mode. Discussions intended to reach a decision can be compared with those intended simply to express what comes to mind and can be juxtaposed. Finally, they can work on role-playing being soft when others are pressing them to be hard, and vice versa, as they progress toward learning how to apply this self-control in more and more realistic, challenging situations.

VII

The distinctions between hard and soft states of being and approaches to communication developed in this chapter have a number of uses for communication educators. The following are some functions of this set of constructs:

a. A means for categorizing and understanding interrelationships among the many units of study or ways of growth that currently are being incorporated within a comprehensive program of communication education

b. A means for countering arguments that any one approach to communicating is better, more necessary, more natural, or more humane than others within this discipline

c. A means for assessing the comprehensiveness of a communication education program to determine the extent to which it provides a balanced set of offerings

d. A means for integrating the somatic, affective, and cognitive dimensions of an episode of communication, to view the participants as organismic wholes not just as word exchangers

e. A means for one to assess individual skills, habit patterns, or propensities in dealing with others to determine the extent to which one is capable of responding appropriately in a full range of circumstances

f. A means for one to assess the kinds of situations most likely to arise in a professional role and one's own or another's suitability for filling that role

g. A means for assessing measuring instruments which evaluate an instructional program for their appropriateness to the program's goals (e.g., a hard scale being used to measure soft objectives) and to design new means of evaluation

h. A means for quickly labelling perceived communication breakdowns in terms of how well suited participants' styles of relating were to one another or to the circumstances of the situation

i. A means for identifying the appropriate circumstances for applying soft vs. hard approaches to relating

j. A means for designing instruction in shifting from one state to the other, in addition to implementing each state once attained.

The constructs hard and soft are not concrete or easily described. They refer to a constellation of factors present to a greater or lesser extent at each moment of human existence. In some instances, as when a golfer is prepared to swing, a diver to jump, a tennis player to serve, these states ought to be in perfect balance for optimal performance. At other times, one state should predominate. It is hoped that in this chapter the characteristics of each state, the circumstances in which each is more appropriate, and the means for switching from one to the other have been described in a way that will prove useful to the communication educator.

CHAPTER 2

Flexibility Training: Developing Communicative Freedom

Instructional Goals

Communication theories and skills usually are viewed as tools with which individuals are equipped to better achieve their interpersonal goals. Presumably, a communication event begins when one perceives a need to affect one's environment in a particular way. In other words, one has a goal: to change someone's mind, to make a friend, to solve a problem, to urge someone to action, etc. Next, a means or a plan for achieving the goal comes to mind and an approach designed to manipulate the situation is put into play. Transactions occur, dialogue proceeds, and the individual gains a sense of satisfaction if his or her aim seems achieved, or a sense of disappointment if the situation turns out other than he or she had hoped.

Communication educators contribute to optimizing effectiveness at each stage in this process. Learners are taught to identify and articulate goals. In fact, considerable stress usually is given to specifying an objective, clarifying a problem, or otherwise zeroing in on the aim for the communicative event. Also, they strive to enlarge and polish students' repertoires of ideas, methods, and skills for achieving their aims, i.e., how to encode verbal and nonverbal messages most likely to have the desired impact on others. Finally, they explain theories and empirically tested propositions about human behavior which are useful in understanding why particular events turn out as they do. This material helps to illuminate the patterns leading to the successes and failures students experience in interaction.

Such an approach to communication training affects students in ways beyond our intent. On the surface it appears to empower them, to make them stronger, more capable persons. However, a more sharply focused examination suggests that a subtle crippling effect may be taking place. Let us look closely at the process being reinforced through this procedure.

Where does a person look to identify his or her communication goals? What is the source of one's answer to the question: "What do I want to achieve in this speech, this course, this relationship, etc.?" Ultimately, one must identify and draw upon one's values, one's vision of the conditions under which one prefers to live. One must say to oneself: "I want to achieve this set of circumstances, this particular situation, and not its opposite." An image or fantasy arises of how one's existence *should* be.

The more attached or committed one is to one's goal, to one's vision, the more energetically that ideal is pursued and other alternatives are avoided. Objects or people who appear useful in achieving that end are seen as allies; other phenomena are seen as irrelevant or as enemies. The individual adopts a discriminating, judgmental stance toward the environment, sorting out the good from the bad, the helpful from the hindering, reacting to each with mounting positive or negative affect. His or her posture toward people and situations becomes an *aggressive* one—they are either welcomed as friends and efforts are made to cling to them and keep them in that state, or they are perceived as hostile and efforts are made to manipulate them into the shape preferred.

In short, the individual is at war with the environment. Life is experienced as a struggle. With every struggle go the fears of losing, the hatred of opponents, the disappointments of setbacks, the resentment of barriers, and the loneliness and alienation of seeing others merely as tools for one's project and oneself as a tool in their efforts, to be discarded when no longer useful.

This process may sound like an election campaign in which the student is a candidate seeking to win over the hearts and minds of voters. Unfortunately, people often see themselves as caught up in such a game. This view may spring from childhood when parents and peers exert pressure on one to shape up to a set of norms, or risk being rejected and powerless. As helpless children conditional caring puts us in the position of being candidates seeking to win others' approval. Most of us learn some strategies that work effectively within the familiar confines of home, neighborhood, and local schools.

Upon being thrust into the world, exposed to unfamiliar, even more competitive contexts, old strategies are less adequate. The influential, approved posture is hard to identify in many situations, and is complex and multidimensional in others. At first, one tends to avoid such settings or feels terribly self-conscious in them. New effort must be made to decipher people's expectations or responses, to reflect afterward on whether or not one has said or done the right things, and to rehearse mentally how to come on more appealingly in the future. One can dislike the people who respond differently because they are the cause of this effort and pain. One can relax with people who readily agree. It is easier, more pleasant, to be with them. Eventually, people are sorted roughly into these two categories, and life is organized to maximize pleasant contacts and to minimize unfamiliar, troublesome ones.

The flow of life, however, won't always allow this arrangement to prevail, and one begins to hope that through some special training one's fears, frustrations, and shyness in many settings might be overcome. So one enrolls in a communication course. The goal: to reduce the experience of bad feelings by learning how to be attractive and potent in situations that now elude one.

Such a goal is in harmony with most teachers' course objectives which are to have students learn what occurs in interpersonal communication and thereby to be more effective. We teach how interpersonal attraction and impression formation work, as well as other theories explaining how people develop their judgments of others and their ideas. We set up exercises in which classmates give feedback about how they see and evaluate one another, what they like and dislike. Students gain insight into others' phenomenal worlds and how their communication styles affect them. They are satisfied with such courses because they become more confident, more able to see and do what others like, i.e., shrewder manipulators of others' reactions.

"But what's the problem?" one might ask. "Students get what they are after, and teachers achieve their course objectives. The transaction is successful!"

In one sense it is, but before judging the outcome, examine what is ultimately achieved. Students still see people essentially in two ways: as approving or disapproving of them and their messages. Their lives are still focused on this struggle. They are more skilled at it, but they remain wary, anxious, and on guard until they feel accepted. They constantly work to prevent this state from slipping away. The know what to show others to gain their approval, but they still must strain to repress impulses or messages from within that might endanger this rapport. They still must seduce pleasant reactions from everyone they meet. They are as trapped, as vulnerable, as at odds with the world, as they were before taking the course, even though they are now better equipped to win the struggle to which they have condemned themselves.

There, of course, is nothing "wrong" with wanting to "win" approval through communication transactions. It is a fine state of affairs between people and even at times worth some pretending to achieve. The danger lies in *identifying* with the part of oneself being likable, thinking oneself to be *only* the mask held up to the world so that it will react positively; when one occasionally fails, "taking it personally," feeling that one's whole being, not just a small part of oneself, is being rejected. This narrow vision of self is like living in one room of a big house and being deceived into thinking that it is the *only* room, so that when the room is invaded, there is nowhere else to go, and one is trapped.

What, therefore, is the source of this dilemma, and what might be the role of a communication instructor in helping students to deal with it?

People are *stuck* in a never-ending cycle as long as they are committed to a win-lose model. The beginning of this wheel is one's self-image. Children fear losing parents' love and care when they stray beyond the limited range of behaviors deemed to be "good." Keeping within this domain is experienced as a matter of life or death. Eventually, their instinct for survival becomes translated into a drive to maintain not the real self, but the self they believe they must be. They come to think of themselves only as that "good child." Cause-effect patterns regarding interaction with others become hardened into *concepts about reality*. They are mired in feeling safe and loved only upon seeing acknowledgment of their "persona" in others' eyes, and feel fear and embarrassment upon being seen otherwise. They feel proud when successful and self-disgust when failing to achieve such responses. What began as a mechanism for coping with a need becomes exalted into a virtue.[1]

In effect, they become *addicted* to being liked, to seeing it as the only way they can feel good; they panic at the threat of being disliked; and they would do almost anything to maintain their positive image. As this identity hardens, other ways of behaving, perhaps being assertive or angry, are eliminated from their behavioral repertoire with internal messages such as "I shouldn't do that . . . ." At times these messages seem justified, but lack of practice or positive experience with alternate responses makes them say, "I can't do that, I'll mess it up," which becomes a self-fulfilling prophecy. The result is that it seems truer to say, "I *have* to be the way I am with others," rather than, "This is the way I *want* to be."

The pattern explored here is not limited to the issue of approval. For some individuals it is a self-image of being aggressive that must be maintained, for others it is being submissive, for others being smart, for others being pretty, for others being "cool." The list is endless among the range of people and within each individual.

This process operates unconsciously, until one stops to reflect on one's existence. Certain questions help to identify the dimensions of self-image that one is struggling to maintain. One is: "Who am I?"[2] The list of adjectives or social roles offered in response to this question defines what an individual is struggling to maintain, what one seeks to affirm in all interpersonal relations. Another question is: "How did I appear in situations that caused me to feel psychic pain or pleasure?" When one feels bad it usually is because a dimension of self-image has been thwarted, or because one appears as one thinks one shouldn't. When one feels good, an aspect of self-image is being applauded or confirmed.

Thus, daily interaction situations are constantly being appraised, and these judgments arouse feelings needed to cope with them. More specifically, one feels fear when a situation seems to be approaching in which one's self-image will be threatened; one feels anger at the apparent cause of that threat. One feels anticipation in advance of a situation that will confirm one's self-image, that will help one feel secure and appreciated; and one feels disappointment when circumstances do not produce this effect. Ambition is working toward a state of ultimate security or support for one's self-image; depression occurs when this direction seems stymied and the energy toward that goal must be smothered. Self-image is a mental construct, but its effect is emotional. Cognition and affect are intertwined.

In communication, the desire to sustain one's own view of self and others' view of self within the perimeters of self-image leads to manipulation, constriction of awareness, and conflict. If I see myself as a set of essential, rigid characteristics or I enter any situation with stiff notions of how it *should* turn out, I then restrict my awareness to factors that seem significant to achieving or threatening myself or my goals. For example, if I must affirm myself as sexy, then I must have women attracted to me. Consequently, I see men as irrelevant and women as available or not, and I repress messages arising in myself that might appear unsexy. If I must affirm myself as righteous, then I must be seen as a "good" person. I see only signs of people's values; I sort them out on the basis of where they stand; I avoid those opposed to me or I try to change their views; and I repress any utterances or behaviors that would appear "evil."[3]

In short, my perception is narrow, my realm of tolerance is narrow, and my available behaviors are narrow. I am consistently susceptible to boredom, resentment, and inhibiting myself. I must work endlessly to appear to myself and to others what I believe I should be. I feel guilty when I fail, arrogant when I succeed; and as the struggle ensues, I often feel tense, constrained, burdened, gloomy, trapped.

Instruction in communication that supports the illusion that the self-image must be protected, that bolsters its defenses without examining what is being preserved, may be doing more harm than good. By armoring the student more deeply against what he or she is trying to avoid, the teacher is encouraging a debilitating endeavor. Essentially, the teacher is sustaining a materialistic contract with life, giving the student the currency with which to "buy" the reactions from others that he or she thinks are needed.[4]

Instead, the function of communication education might be viewed as eliminating illusory needs, as expanding the students' sense of his or her own freedom. In this approach the student loses or gives up what pens him or her in, rather than simply accumulating more self-protective information. By surrendering an attachment to the self-image, the student gradually is awakened to the vast realm of possibilities in self-expression and in reactions from others from which he or she has been defending the self. When one sees the ways of being to which one has been limited and the needlessness for avoiding their opposites (i.e., the groundlessness of one's fears), one will gain a new sense of flexibility, of communicative freedom.

If one learns that it is possible to survive intact after appearing foolish as well as smart, hostile as well as pleasant, plain as well as attractive, clumsy as well as competent, etc., one is then liberated from the encumbrance of self-image, from childhood restraints, from the masks one has been holding up, from the daily struggle for psychic survival.

As one becomes reacquainted with aspects of self and others that have been avoided, one can learn how to transmute energies that had been feared into healthy, enriching forces. For one student, his or her anger and the anger of others can be seen as means for cutting through complacency, for sharp reminders of what is being overlooked, for swift explication of what lies at the heart of a conflict—instead of as death blows to a relationship. For another, warmth can be seen as an expression of caring, of unity, of respect—instead of as a smothering, grasping, sticky way of ensuring commitment. Students thus accept as friends parts of their beings which they had seen as enemies. The more dimensions of themselves that they accept, the less energy they put into discriminating, pretending, and manipulating; the more porous and flexible their self-image becomes, the more they will relax in daily discourse; the more fully they can energize their potential for full humanness and self-actualization, the stronger and more grown up they will feel.

In fact, as more and more of the limits on self are cut away, one finds that there is no need to cling to any particular definition of self or behavioral model. One can answer the question, "Who are you?" with a shrug of the shoulders and a smile. This dropping away of all ego definitions is a dimension of the state of "enlightenment," the highest attainment of Buddhist and other mystical practices.[5] At first, this total openness may seem like a state of chaos without form or direction or any ethical limits. Quite the contrary. When nothing within or outside oneself is seen as vile or threatening, because there is no one, no ego, to be defended, then everything is appreciated for what it is—loved, cherished, seen with deep compassion, with utter understanding and acceptance.

One's religious expression changes from prayers of supplication to prayers of gratitude for life as it is. One's behavior is no longer striving for anything outside, but flows from within and takes form much as a child or lover or artist or scientist or carpenter or anyone acts when most deeply absorbed in daily tasks, doing them with energy, discipline and dedication for their own sake, not as a means for achieving extrinsic goals. One participates in daily life as a member of the Rockefeller family works at a job, not because he or she needs the rewards to be obtained at the end, but for the joy and challenge of the effort itself. Being "rich" is merely a state in which a person is content with what one has, whether one has one dollar or ten million dollars; this state of mind, this contentment with the here and now, can be extended to every dimension of an interpersonal relationship. If I can accept how I am and how people see me, I am rich and free from striving to impress them or myself.

The stifling effect of maintaining one's self-image is seen vividly in the phenomenon of stage fright, speech anxiety, or reticence. The fantasy of being seen by others in a way unacceptable to oneself causes inhibition of verbalization, emotional distress, and various physiological symptoms. In a given situation, this impasse can be overcome by building the speaker's confidence in his or her power to achieve the desired impact and to avoid the feared one. Or, it can be *dissolved* by helping him or her to see that there is really nothing to lose upon "failing," except a constricted self-image. The lyric "Freedom's just another word for nothing left to lose" could serve as a theme for this approach to relieving speech anxiety and for this whole approach to instruction as well.

An important lesson in this process is that problems are never solved so long as they are attacked aggressively. Whatever "solution" is forced simply creates a different situation and new problems. For example, getting a divorce doesn't "solve the problem" of a bad marriage, both people just face new kinds of problems. The issue that broke up their relationship is only really settled when each partner looks at what he or she couldn't endure in the other person or self and understands and melts his or her resistance to it. Otherwise, each is forever locked in a lifetime struggle to find or to avoid that characteristic in another person. They aren't free of each other at all.

A loving relationship in which areas of tension are acknowledged, faced, and worked through (until one or both people let go of their need to perform or reject the offending behavior) is on far more solid ground than one in which there is an agreement, spoken or covert, to outlaw any dimension of human action, or each tries to mold the other to suit his or her desires.[6] Trying to manipulate situations endlessly in order to achieve perfect happiness is doomed to failure. Working with the pain caused by the gaps between reality and one's needs, acknowledging those spaces and working with them internally seems more promising in bringing peace of mind.

From this posture, painful, disappointing situations are seen as clues to what we need to work on not as incidents to put out of one's mind or forget. They indicate addiction, that we have been deprived of something we think we need. Instead of avoiding such situations or placating or tyrannizing others to do what we want, we confront such moments, think them through, discuss them with the others involved or with friends to explore how we were stuck, how our identities were threatened.[7] These are the ripest, juiciest moments of existence. The more aware we are of our restraints, the closer we are to being free of them. These are opportunities to "cleanse the doors of perception"; they are mirrors with which to see ourselves, and to expand our flexibility and freedom.[8]

An unexpectedly disappointing experience opens one up to lowering one's defenses, to surrendering an attachment to old ways of relating to people, and to exploring new possibilities, new rooms in one's inner house. This openness can take the form of a sudden burst of temper from a "normally" placid person, a gush of softheartedness from a hard businessman, etc. Or, it may force someone to involuntarily give up usual routines and use this step "backward" to see life from a broader perspective. This process is at the heart of all religious practices that mandate rituals, sabbaths, services, meditation, and other vacations from daily life.[9] These forced surrenderings of habit put one, albeit unwillingly, outside everyday strivings the better to see them in perspective. Unexpected, jolting experiences that do not bring anticipated rewards also serve momentarily to shatter hardened, rigid mental maps about how life works. These periods of frustration, of groping about for new ways to get oneself "together" again leave gaps in which new ideas can flourish.[10] At times like these, one is not "full" of schemes for manipulating the world; there is room to entertain a fresh perspective. The approach advocated here requires a turnaround in thinking, a movement which needs inner space, openness and willingness to try on another way of seeing reality.[11]

One's task in life becomes transformed from trying to create a life-style in which all one's needs are met to working with whatever blocks one from dealing with reality as it is; from trying to be safe, to trying to take more risks; from frantically trying to fulfill every childhood ambition to ridding the self of them and thereby lightening one's load.

An extraordinarily effective means for diminishing the encumbering power of a goal is to focus attention on it. A period of thoroughly articulating exactly what a person wants from an ideal job, mate, friendship, etc., and exploring how realistic and how really necessary those ambitions are, often ends in viewing those lofty aims with less attachment and with a greater sense of humor. The humor comes from seeing oneself as a child concentrating only on grasping for the brass ring, instead of enjoying the carousel ride itself. This posture is not only humorous. Most tragic literature includes a narrative in which such absurd prideful yearnings cause the downfall of the protagonist.[12]

We are constantly passing from level to level of yearning or self-image attachment in the normal process of maturation. Once, I *had* to have a neater toy than my friend, now that *need* seems childish. At one time or another I *had* to appear tough, cool, handsome, talented, affluent, clever to my friends. Each need passed away, only to be replaced by a more sophisticated one. As long as this absurd progression of personal ambitions goes on, I am a victim of my pride and my passions. To become free, the struggle must shift from meeting to quieting down or seeing through these desires themselves (and ultimately this "desire" for freedom must be dropped, as well).

When one looks hard at what bothers one, when one experiences it fully as it happens rather than thrashing about trying to escape or prevent it, one comes to know it fully, to make friends with it. In this way one learns to live with one's desires, to reown one's freedom to continue or discontinue one's struggle. He or she senses an ability to choose, takes responsibility for one's efforts, detaches the self from identifying with them and is in control of them, rather than allowing them to control the self.

Students' awareness, released from having to focus on specific goals and dangers, will expand in scope and clarity. The need to structure situations will decline and, since there is less to fear or resent, the points at which conflict with others usually arises can be transformed into moments of adventure and learning. Instead of grasping for routines or strategies to achieve predetermined goals, their dialogue with others will be experienced as improvisations yielding surprising, unpredictable results.

Of course, this direction for instruction is not necessarily a smooth, easily travelled path. In fact, it may be more difficult than traditional approaches to course work in this discipline. This thrust introduces a new notion of what more "advanced" study in communication can be—not necessarily involving acquisition of more and more information and techniques, but, instead, cutting away more deeply at the internal structures upon which communication difficulties are based.

This approach to communication education is not at all a new one. The illusory and limiting nature of the self-image, or ego, has been a fundamental principle of Oriental psychology for thousands of years. In Western thought, the "third force," humanistic psychology movement, includes a variety of systems for enlarging one's view of one's own potential. The process developed in both these schools can be applied in the direction outlined in this chapter.[13]

Instructional Methods

If we view one's potential as full use of one's moment-to-moment perceptual and expressive energies, and we view self-image as a limiting, funneling brake on these energies, then three major instructional approaches (and combinations thereof) seem applicable for returning one's innate communicative freedom. The first is to *heighten awareness* of what is happening, of one's current mode of relating and of what (and how) one is excluding from one's experience. The second is to *relieve the anxiety* or loosen the barriers that block more energies from coming in or going out of the organism. The third is to stimulate or *energize* the dimensions being repressed (or avoided) to allow them to flow more freely with less inhibition. Several specific instructional techniques subsumed under each of these approaches are given. Each is described very briefly. Other sources must be consulted for a full understanding of each process mentioned.

I. Awareness

    A. The most basic process is simple awareness of one's mind as it schemes in behalf of the self-image, a traditional means for which is *meditation*—insight meditation or being an impartial witness to one's thoughts (as opposed to systems of meditation seeking *samadhi* which suggest another focus of attention such as a *mantra*). The thoughts observed rising and receding in the mind provide vivid clues to the images of self to which the meditator is attached.[14]

    B. Nonjudgmental awareness of one's stream of consciousness is also an aim of verbal *free association* employed in psychoanalysis. Recently, the process of *reevaluation* or co-counseling has stressed the value of simply being aware of whatever comes to mind and sharing this awareness with another person, not necessarily a trained therapist.[15] Expressing one's uncensored flow of thoughts in writing, as well as orally, via the traditional form of a diary or a *journal*, is a medium that has been elaborated to maximize its usefulness as a means of self-awareness by psychologist Ira Progoff.[16]

    C. A more pointed, direct way to identify the outlines of the self-image is responding to specific revealing questions[17] such as:

        1. Who am I?
        2. Who are the significant others in my life? What dimensions of self do I reveal to each? What do they do in response that brings me pleasure?[18]
        3. What would I want to avoid saying or doing with each person? How would I hate to appear to each person?
        4. What kinds of people do I avoid? What do they do or trigger in me that I resist?[19]

5. What are some alternatives to the ways in which I deal with the people in my life? What might be the consequences of each alternative?[20]
6. If I had only one last opportunity to see these people again what might I say to them?[21]
7. How do I and our relationship appear from their point of view? How are they trying to manipulate me in order to maintain their own self-image?[22]
8. Other less direct questions, called *koans*, are used by Zen masters to aid in breaking students' images of themselves (e.g., "What was your original face, the face you had before your mother and father were born?").[23]

D. Exploring the historical development of the dimensions of self-image can heighten awareness. By recalling all of one's memories of others' reactions to a specific characteristic, the nature and power of the limitation can be better understood. This is what women have been doing recently in consciousness-raising groups. Any dimension of self-image can be explored in this way by writing a slice of an autobiography, e.g., the story of "a neat appearance" or "not yelling" or "competitiveness," etc., in my life.[24]

E. Talking with others who experience similar self-image limits can provide fresh awareness into one's predicament. Sharing with someone in a position like one's own, especially one who has transcended the limit and opened the self in new directions, can be illuminating and inspiring.[25] An essential part of this process is the model or mirror provided by the other. Seeing your dynamics in someone else allows for some distance or detachment which makes objective awareness less painful, more clear and fruitful. A work of art, such as a play, a novel, a short story, or a poem occasionally reflects one's own image in bold relief. Characters in fiction can serve as silent partners in whom one sees oneself more clearly. This is an especially valuable approach, since in fiction characters are often depicted as being drawn into intense conflict situations due to unquenchable self-image demands that are virtually universal, such as pride, power, and love. In addition, stories or tales told by religious teachers of Sufi, Hassidic, Zen, and other traditions also serve to reflect to the reader a clearer vision of one's own truncated thinking.[26]

F. When one first views a person or a situation, one sees it purely, with pristine awareness, and then quickly categorizes the elements and appraises them according to one's desire system or self-image. A goal of this work is to extend that moment of first awareness in order to make it more basic to one's view of reality, to maximize the freshness, astonishment, and wonder with which situations are perceived. Progress toward this end comes from methods of sensory awareness, which are exercises designed to bring participants "out of their minds" and "to come to their senses."[27]

G. Taking time out from the usual patterns of daily life can provide the distance or detachment with which to view these patterns more objectively and to place them in meaningful perspective. This can be a function of an annual vacation or a weekly day of rest (the Sabbath). At a greater extreme, and hence more potent, is an experience in which one views one's life from the perspective of the ultimate break in routine, death. Contact with the inevitable reality of dying can cast new light on how fully one's life is being lived.[28]

II. Relieving Anxiety

A. Mind and body work together; they are interdependent. The psychic tension that mounts when one's self-image is threatened is accompanied by somatic tension and is relieved as the body relaxes. In a relaxed state one's "guard is down" and new ways of being become more possible. Hence, when one meets new situations while *physically relaxed*, they need not elicit avoidance, repression, or a conditioned response. Biofeedback, Jacobsen's system of relaxation, and *t'ai-chi-ch'uan* are methods that have been used to face previously tense situations in an open, flowing, hence flexible, way.[29] Similarly, hatha-yoga, massage, and *aikido* are ways of freeing the flow of energy through the body, thereby loosening the bonds of anxiety.[30] Systems of meditation which demonstrably relax body and mind (such as transcendental meditation), as well as other systems which alter the state of consciousness, thereby resting or setting aside customary inhibitions or tensions, fit in this category. The latter systems include alcohol, marijuana, and physical activities such as athletics, whirling, chanting, etc.[31]

B. Anxiety about the future or the past takes attention away from what is going on at the moment and vice versa. Hence, ways of being more aware, more mindful of what is occurring in the here and now serve to reduce anxiety. Becoming more awake to and conscious of everyday activities such as breathing, eating, or walking, is often a first step toward being present-centered in more complex situations such as face-to-face relating in an emotion-laden situation.[32]

C. Anxiety is also relieved in an atmosphere that seems free of judgment, where a natural informality and "anything goes" value system prevail. *Retreat* learning centers (such as Esalen and Bethel, Maine) are cultural islands where explorations beyond the typical limits of the self-image seem to flow more freely.[33] Any time a context is established wherein people are encouraged to discuss their inhibitions or to try new behaviors without evaluative feedback, an *anxiety-relieving setting* exists. Examples include the simulation game, the T-group, the consciousness-raising group, an acting class, or any situation in which the likelihood of embarrassment is reduced and personal experimentation is supported.[34]

D. Moving out of a laboratory or learning context and into real-life experience can be facilitated with a minimum of anxiety by a graduated sequencing of risk as employed in deconditioning behavior modification programs. Taking small steps out of one's usual realm and experiencing success with them can be a way of breaking out of self-image binds with a minimum of fear.[35] This principle of using rewarding, successful goal achievement is a key part of "reality therapy" as well.[36]

E. Clinging to what seems essential in one's self-image and the fear of losing it can be reduced by doing without that cherished act for a while. Moderate forms of asceticism, such as not talking for a day or longer, shutting off a sense (e.g., as in a "blind walk"), fasting, backpacking in the wilderness, nonaction (via meditation), and related methods, can help an individual do without or let go of something which had been deemed essential to one's well-being.

F. Anxiety about releasing the self-image can also be somewhat reduced by reading the works of those who advocate it, either Eastern sources dealing with Buddhism or Taoism or Western writers in the school of humanistic psychology. In this method of personal change, the anxious mind is talking itself out of its own self-imposed limits by contact with powerful liberating ideas that are well articulated.

III. Energizing Avoided Areas

A. If a heretofore censored dimension of self is identified and given a voice, then it can break through one's habitual armor and find expression. Upon being aired, its actual impact can be experienced, instead of merely imagined. Usually the outcome of such a first step is gratifying, lending credence to the theory that a fully functioning self is more rewarding then a stifled one. Sidney Jourard stresses the value of disclosing areas of the self usually kept under wraps.[37] The Gestalt therapist is always on the alert for nonverbal clues to areas of a client's inner and outer reality that are being avoided; his goal is attending to them and reintegrating them into a more comprehensive view of self.[38] The process of verbally expressing disowned parts of the self is carried to an extreme in primal scream therapies which ask clients to go back into the distant past to recall and discharge feelings withheld because of feared rejection.[39]

38

B. Aspects of self which are usually inhibited also can be given energy through physical action. In the encounter group feelings which are repressed or sugarcoated with words are often given room for release nonverbally. Thus, hugs, arm wrestling, trust falls, group break-ins and breakouts are all ways of doing with the body what someone can't or won't express adequately with words.[40] An even more vigorous and thorough system for releasing blocked messages through loosening body tensions, called bio-energetics, has been developed by Alexander Lowen.[41] In and of itself, nonverbal contact is a realm of behavior that many people exclude from self. These exercises help return this rich body language to the realm of possibility.

C. Another vehicle for encouraging the release of messages held in by a solid self-image is symbolic imagery. Some people can express their deepest feelings more vividly through art, music, dance, poetry, mime, film and other creative media. These are universal means for self-expression that are now being applied widely as ways for non-artists to articulate aspects of their being that have no other daily outlet.[42]

The integration of these methods into a course plan is beyond the scope of this chapter. A few guidelines for this synthesis might be noted, however. First, the student should be helped to develop individual learning goals and a plan for achieving them, rather than be pulled through the instructor's course objectives. Despite the aids described in this chapter, the path for personal growth can be extremely arduous; it requires genuine, deeply felt inner motivation to work at it conscientiously. The spur of grades is insufficient. Second, the learning must be active, experiential. To be absorbed deeply enough to make a difference, learning experiences must engage as much of the student's organism as possible. Third, the instructor must take the approach seriously enough to apply it to himself or herself and be engaged in the same learning process as the student. Then each will open up to the other as widely, as deeply, as genuinely as they can at the moments of contact. Nothing is more discouraging to a person first thawing an image of self than to be working with a guide who is frozen in his or her own being. Nothing is more exhilarating than a teaching-learning process that is a mutual expansion toward greater personal freedom.

In all of the ways mentioned, and in many others, the walls within which one is confined by self-image can be pulled down. Then, instead of defending those barriers and perceiving only the weapons of opponents, an individual can become aware and available to the broad vista of the moment-to-moment environment. People will seem less threatening as one has less to protect. One can use the information offered by the communication teacher to explore and to play confidently and joyfully in one's world, not to deter or defeat it. This spontaneous, flexible, free mode of relating can begin in the classroom and expand outward until it is an available posture even in the marketplaces of our society.

CHAPTER 3

Objectives, Evaluation, and Grading: An Experiential Perspective

I

Too often innovations in education are used as solutions for problems to which they are not suited. Most recently behavioral objectives and quantitative rating systems have been advocated for improving instruction in speech.[1] Although originating in other disciplines, these procedures are considered directly applicable to the teaching of interpersonal communication. Such proposals, however, ignore characteristics inherent in this field of study which have clear implications for how it should be taught.

A student might enter a class in history completely ignorant of the events which occurred in the period to be studied. Consequently, what one student gains from the course can and perhaps should be comparable to what all members of the class learn. In contrast, a student enters a class in interpersonal communication with a lifetime of related experiences and many deeply embedded attitudes about his or her participation in that process. In fact, each student has a *unique* life history. No two people grow up under identical conditions. Each one has contacted an individual network of significant others who have shaped his or her thinking and behavior when relating to others.

In addition, at the moment of taking the communication class, each student has his or her own specific relationships to which he or she would like to apply what is being learned. Students in a history class, on the other hand, to apply what they have learned, can each pick up the same newspaper and relate the past they have explored to present political events which affect all of them almost uniformly. Each student in the interpersonal communication class is in a unique position vis-à-vis family, friends, and others with whom he or she relates. Any transfer of learning must be adapted to his or her particular situation.

Similarly, the careers which students anticipate can have distinct communication needs. Doctors, lawyers, and Indian chiefs all need to know basic math. But, when communicating, doctors have a greater need to be therapeutic, lawyers to be persuasive, and Indian chiefs, I imagine, need skill in group leadership. Thus, the futures they foresee affect the relevance of students' study in communication.

In sum, all students have different pasts, presents, and futures which influence deeply how they perceive and react to their experiences in studying interpersonal communication. Such a characteristic places this field of study in sharp contrast to virtually all other fields in the educational spectrum. The distinction must be prominent when examining objectives and a system of evaluation in this field.

Nevertheless, one might say that individualistic goals should be overlooked, that students should be forced, despite preexisting biases, to explore all principles and practices of human relations. After all, a survey approach is taken in the study of literature, about which students also bring some preferences to class. Here again, however, another distinctive characteristic of oral communication makes such an analogy inappropriate.

Choices among works of literature can be made at leisure while browsing in a library; a book may be picked up and put down at will; an idea about literature may be jotted down in class and then retrieved even years later when the need arises. Oral interaction, however, must be dealt with as it occurs; interpersonal crises cannot be initiated, interrupted, or terminated at will; what is learned must be employed in conversations spontaneously, as things happen, without the opportunity to rely on notes or other external sources of information.

These differences have direct implications. Knowledge or skills to be applied with such immediacy must be learned deeply; they must be thoroughly internalized in order to be brought to bear at the instant they are needed. This kind of learning demands complete *commitment* to the goals of the experience, a clear sense of their worth and meaning to oneself. In addition, this kind of learning should be conducted via experiences closely comparable to its ultimate use, that is *experientially*, through actual in-and-out-of-class conversations.

To expect students to be thoroughly committed and involved in such learning experiences which seem irrelevant to them is foolish. Nothing is gained but forced compliance. Only a method whereby students can participate in tasks molded to individual needs is suited to learning in interpersonal communication.

The need for individualization, commitment, and active involvement in this field of learning suggests that a fresh look at some common assumptions about objectives, evaluation, and grading procedures is in order.

II

Currently, much attention is being given to the development of behavioral objectives. These are intended to eliminate subjectivity in grading. They allow one to evaluate behavior, knowledge, and/or attitudes with respect to fixed standards. In other words, the teacher asks, "How close does this student come to what is ideal, to achieving concrete objectives?" The answer to this question relies upon a set of absolute, objective, or categorical goals.[2]

The first step in developing such goals is to define the "ideal" communicator, what he or she does, what he or she knows, and what he or she believes. Does such a person exist? Most definitely not. No person *always* is effective in interpersonal relations. No one is consistently understood, persuasive, entertaining, helpful, etc. Every individual has specific skills which are somewhat effective in the situations he or she faces, and these situations are ones that only he or she faces.

The variables in any given situation include the personality, age, status, ethnic background, etc., of the persons involved, the kind of task being undertaken, the setting, the time available, and other considerations. These vary from incident to incident, and the patterns which recur vary according to the overall life situation of each individual.

Generalizations which may be applied to *all* possible interpersonal encounters necessarily are highly abstract. To recite them is meaningless. The ability to recognize their relevance at a particular moment and to apply them spontaneously characterizes an effective communicator. The appropriateness of the application is crucial and varies from occasion to occasion.

Perhaps math problems always have single right answers; some theorems apply to all related instances, but communication situations are too varied and complex to allow for an ideal against which individuals might be judged. Categorical behavioral, cognitive, or affective objectives cannot be validly used, therefore, as a basis for instruction or evaluation in an interpersonal communication course.

What then can one rely on to guide instruction if such goals are excluded? How can individual differences be accommodated in a single curriculum? I stated earlier that learning in this discipline should be *experiential*. Although students differ dramatically in *what* they need or want to learn, they share substantial common ground in *how* they go about learning. In other words, one might need an infinite number of statements to create a universally relevant set of content objectives for a course in interpersonal communication, but would need only a few objectives to establish an *experience*-based curriculum. There are countless things a person might do or know about communicating, but a limited number of ways to learn more about this process.

42

Consequently, I suggest employing experiential, instead of categorical, objectives. Such objectives define what a student will do in order to learn, not what the learning will produce. Perhaps the distinction can be clarified with an example. If a text is required in a course, a categorical or behavioral objective might be: "The student will be able to identify the ten major ideas in the text on a true-false test." An experiential goal for the same experience might be: "The student will read the text, identify the ideas most relevant to his or her current relationships, and write an informal paper on how they might be applied." The former objective assures the teacher that the student will learn what the teacher wants learned; the latter assures that the student will learn something deemed relevant by the student.[3]

The first step in planning an effective course in interpersonal communication, therefore, is to establish a set of experiential goals that are most likely to evoke personally meaningful student learning. To do so, one does not search the professional literature in the field to determine the latest speculations regarding what everyone should know. Instead, all the learning *resources* available in and out of the classroom are matched with possible *ways* of learning to create a series of experiences with optimal potential for student growth. Resources differ according to the materials, institution, and community available to the teacher, but some ways of learning are common to nearly all students.[4] Several are described briefly:

1. Students can learn by *observing* others communicate. Social comparison research has shown that people learn many behavioral patterns from models, from watching others interact. In the classroom, students can observe others talking; outside they can be asked to visit and observe people in situations similar to those in which they would like to improve.

2. Students can learn by *practicing* the communication behaviors that interest them. Engaging in an activity can generate insights into what that activity involves. Role-playing in the classroom employs this principle. Students can actually carry out activities outside the classroom in which they would like to improve and then report what they learned from them.

3. Students can learn by receiving *feedback* from others about their communication behavior. Classroom observers can provide this, or it can be offered in a modified T-group where uninhibited feedback is encouraged. Outside of class, students can be asked to interview trusted friends about how they are seen as communicators.

4. Students can learn from *introspection*, or reconsideration of past or imagined situations. Much can be gained by tying together and gleaning the meaning from one's past experiences—psychotherapists nearly all use this tool. Imagined or fantasized situations also yield clues to self-awareness.

5. Students can learn by manipulating what interests them *creatively*. When one draws a model or writes a story or play about a communication situation, one can gain a clearer picture of what is occurring.

6. Students can learn by *teaching* someone else what one already knows, for in that process one is likely to grow to better understand and use whatever is being taught.

7. Students can learn from *secondary sources* of information, i.e., reading articles, listening to lectures, interviewing experts, or in any other way benefiting from the experiences and ideas of others.

These are alternative ways of learning which can be applied to inter-personal communication. This list is not all-inclusive, other approaches could be added. Keeping these in mind, however, the teacher can begin charting a course for any given semester. The first step would be to identify a series of experiential goals to pursue. Many more are conceivable than can be accomplished in a single semester. The process of delimitation should follow laying out an overall set of acceptable alternatives. With these in mind, selection of those actually pursued can be shared by the students who will engage in them.

A sample set of some general experiential goals for a course in interpersonal communication might include a combination of some of the following:

1. Each student will use *introspection* to identify and report:
   a) Current outside relationships which are satisfactory and those in need of improvement
   b) Recent situations in which he/she has been particularly pleased with the communication that occurred and other situations that were particularly frustrating
   c) How individual relationships with others have changed over the years since early childhood
   d) The kinds of communication challenges he/she expects to face in the years ahead
   e) What he/she would like to learn in this course, what is being learned as the course progresses, and a summary of what has been learned at the semester's end.

2. Each student will use *observation* to identify and report:
   a) Behaviors of other students concerning specific group dynamics variables (e.g., participation, influence, norms, etc.) as they engage in small group discussions
   b) Communication behaviors of people performing a job which the student might some day have

c) Communication behaviors of people in situations comparable to those in which the student would like to improve.

3. Each student will *practice* and report what was learned from:
   a) Participating in various kinds of dyads and group discussions in class
   b) Role-playing in class situations which he/she would like to learn how to handle better
   c) Trying to change communication behavior in the out-of-school relationship(s) he/she wants to improve.

4. Each student will obtain *feedback* and report what was learned by:
   a) Observing his/her own behavior in a videotaped group discussion
   b) Listening to observers' reports on his/her behavior in a classroom group discussion
   c) Interviewing a trusted friend about his/her view of the student's communication behavior in specific kinds of situations.

5. Each student will *creatively*:
   a) Write a short story or play, with self as the central character, depicting a situation in which he or she wishes to improve communication ability
   b) Write a poem, make a drawing, or take some photographs that depict feelings experienced when communicating in a specific situation.

6. Each student will try *teaching* someone about interpersonal communication by:
   a) Interviewing another student about a communication difficulty he or she is experiencing and trying to help him or her think it through
   b) Creating a game or exercise which would help someone to learn an important skill in communication.

7. Each student will explore and report what can be learned from *secondary sources* by:
   a) Reading one book or several articles from a recommended bibliography
   b) Interviewing someone whose communication ability he or she admires
   c) Identifying a series of questions about communication which are of interest and asking several people to answer them
   d) Analyzing a scene from a fictional work or biography which has a scene comparable to an experience in the student's life.

Once a set of these and other equally valuable alternatives has been laid out, the teacher must decide how to present them to students and how to evaluate and grade their work.

III

Courses in speech ought to be universally enjoyed. After all, students share ideas of their choosing with classmates and the teacher provides assistance with a clearly vital and potentially very satisfying act—communication. Yet in practice this venture consistently is marred by the anticipation of a letter or number of chilling impact.

The grade often influences the choice of course by the student and the choice of content by the teacher long before the class begins. The grade affects the focus of student attention in the classroom; and in teacher-student dialogue, the grade usually has the last word of the semester. In fact, its influence can linger long after the course content is forgotten.

My purpose is not to attack grading. It is accepted here as an unavoidable, if undesirable, reality to which one may adapt in more or less beneficial ways. I am proposing an approach to evaluation, and subsequently to grading, which encourages rather than frustrates student learning.

The traditional means for evaluating students is comparative. Individual achievement is compared to that of others in the class or grade level; a determination is made of how one's work compares with the work of others, and praise or criticism and a grade are given on that basis.

I have already discussed in detail how inappropriate it is to generalize about or to compare students in regard to their interpersonal communication. An additional factor, peculiar to this subject area, makes such comparisons self-defeating. Whenever students are aware that comparisons are being made among them in an effort to determine suitable grades, a *competitive* system is set up. This becomes especially keen among those whose grades will influence career plans. Competition in other subject area classes may occasionally stimulate increased learning, but in an interpersonal communication course it is almost always destructive.

Here, more than in any other class, students must use one another for learning. Interaction and feedback in the class must be as honest and open as possible. Information about communication behaviors of students and how they are perceived must flow freely among them for maximum learning to occur. Thus, *cooperation* is to be sought and competition discouraged. This demands that each student be evaluated and graded on what he or she alone does, regardless of the performance of others.

The mechanism I have used to meet this criterion is a "contract." Specific tasks, such as those mentioned in the sample experiential goals cited earlier, are suggested, and the student's evaluation and grade are based on individual performance of such tasks. Nevertheless, every evaluation system must make distinctions based on some kind of standard. I have already rejected the possibility of using fixed behavioral objectives. The approach advocated here implies the use of experiential standards.

A basic tenet of this approach is that whatever learning the student gains from the experiences undertaken is OK. The only enforced restriction is that he or she indeed perform a basic set of potentially productive assignments. The contract, therefore, includes a grading system based on

46

how much a student does, not on *what* is learned from the work. The more energy invested in the course, the more work done, the more learning gained from the course, the higher the grade should be.

This approach implies a standard of quantity of experience, not quality. It suggests a way of measuring how much the student experiences. However, the student also deserves evaluation or feedback from the teacher on how well he or she has done based on the teacher's greater experience and knowledge. How can this be done without judging what is important for the student to learn? Here, again, the criterion of experiencing should be paramount.

The teacher's evaluation should be based only on an estimate of how thoroughly the student made use of the experience. Did the student draw the maximum number of inferences from observations, practice, feedback, introspection, etc.? The teacher cannot judge the validity of what the student learned from them, but can make statements about the *process* of learning. He/she can point out significant omissions, overgeneralizations, misunderstandings, etc.; can raise questions about issues that seem to have been overlooked or oversimplified; can praise obviously painstaking effort and subtle insights; and can suggest further sources of information and activities.

Such an evaluation cannot be simplified into a letter or number grade. It can take either of two forms: a grade of "satisfactory" with identification of specific points that seem outstanding, or a grade of "unsatisfactory" with questions or suggestions for additional work to make the experience more productive.

In sum, the procedure for evaluating students' work in interpersonal communication should be to comment upon how well the experience was used for learning, and the procedure for grading should be based on how much effort was given to undertaking potentially worthwhile experiences. These assessments should be made on the basis of a contract including a variety of experiential tasks all likely to lead to learning relevant to each student's own communicative needs. The work, the evaluation, and the grade are to be based on what the individual student did, regardless of what others in the class may have done.

Such a system has several inherent advantages. Requirements for each grade are made clear at the start. The student can approach the work knowing that conclusions reached can be related to his or her own view of the world, they need not please the teacher. The student need only decide how much energy he or she wishes to invest in the course. One sets one's own goal, chooses the most meaningful tasks from the options available, and carries them out thoroughly. If any are deemed inadequate, one learns how to improve and resubmit them.

Within this system three kinds of students who are often discouraged in speech classes can succeed: the rebel, often a member of a minority group, because one can chart one's own course and reach one's own destination; the reticent or shy student because one can do each task at one's own level of readiness to interact (in fact, this technique was first developed in a course for students with speech anxiety); and the nonverbal student because test-taking ability is not at stake here—assignments can be deemed satisfactory even if results are reported briefly and in nonstandard grammar, as long as they have been carried out fully through oral discourse.

IV

In my ten years of experience using contracts as the basis for evaluation and grading in interpersonal communication courses, several guidelines have emerged as most helpful and are listed. Each is followed by an example or application from my own experience.

1. Create a comprehensive list of learning experiences, all of which are relevant to the course you plan to teach.

   Example: A sample list of (rather abstractly defined) experiences was provided earlier; more specific ones are detailed in this section.

2. Decide on a minimum set of experiences that would most likely cover the basic essentials of the course.

   Example: In a college level course I have set the following as my minimum standards:

   a) Regular attendance
   b) Introspective essays—at the beginning of the course: "The relationships in my life to which I would like to apply what I learn this semester and how I would like to improve them"; midway in the course: "What have I learned so far that is most important to me, what do I hope to learn in the time remaining, what will I do to accomplish my goals?" and at the end of the course: "What have I learned this semester that I can apply in my everyday life?"
   c) Read the text and write informal statements on each chapter relating its ideas to your experiences in and out of class this semester.
   d) Keep a weekly log in which you enter the most meaningful thoughts, feelings, and experiences related to human relations that have occurred to you each week in and out of class.

   Students who complete all these tasks are guaranteed a C for the course.

3. Describe additional assignments which can earn students higher grades. These can require more complex cognitive responses, more intensely personal responses, more creative responses, or expose the student to a wider range of learning resources.

   Example: Some sample assignments which involve a variety of approaches to experiential learning are provided here.

a) It can be worthwhile to explore what experts have to say about issues in interpersonal communication that interest you. Find or ask me to recommend three discussions of any topic, and after reading them:
   (1) Cite the three sources.
   (2) Explain in what fundamental ways all agree.
   (3) Point out how they differ.
   (4) Summarize the particular material from these sources that was most meaningful to you.

b) Pair up with another person in your group and make a date to interview each other. Every person is in a great many relationships at once. For example, at some time in one's life a person may be a parent to a child and a child to a parent. Each is quite a different role, yet each is an important part of the person. Encourage your partner to share with you, in depth, how he or she feels, what he or she thinks and does in human relations while carrying out the following roles which apply:

child	friend	student	roommate
sibling	mate or date	parent	consumer
		employee	citizen

   Write a brief and fair summary of the person interviewed, and give it to your partner. Write a brief reaction to the summary written about you, and turn it in with the summary.

c) Pair up with a person in your group and share your answers to the following questions:
   (1) What were our first impressions of each other?
   (2) How have we seen each other as understanding listeners?
   (3) How have we seen each other as being open about our feelings and reactions?
   (4) How have we seen each other support attempts to be open and honest?
   (5) How have we seen each other as able to confront when conflict exists?
   (6) In what ways is each of us outstanding and poor in human relations? What should we do about our needs in this area?
   (7) What is the state or our relationship?

   Write as brief a summary of your dialogue as does it justice, and give it to your partner. Write a brief reaction to the summary you receive, and turn them in together.

d) Plan a specific instance in which you will use the concepts dealt with in this course in your everyday life. Do it and then evaluate your experience in the light of your objectives for this inter-action.
   (1) Describe the person or group with whom or in which you would like to change your behavior.

49

(2) Describe your habitual thoughts, feelings, or behaviors with the person or group.

(3) Describe how you would like to respond ideally.

(4) Describe what a realistic first step might be in growing toward this ideal.

(5) Try it out in reality.

(6) Evaluate it.

(7) Make a plan for a next step.

e) We learn our modes of communicating largely from the people around us, i.e., via observation. Therefore, it might be useful to determine some way of observing people communicating in situations in which you are interested. You may find people doing something you admire in a classroom, where they live, at an informal gathering place, etc. Decide where you are most likely to see what you want. Try to observe at least two examples of this situation. Prepare a list of things to look for and a way to record this information while observing (or afterward). Summarize the results of your observations.

f) An issue raised in this course may cause you some puzzlement. If so, it might be useful to discuss it with people you know. Select three to five people whose opinions you respect, for the following activities:

(1) List several questions you'd like answered by all of them. Ask them to write their answers or ask them orally and summarize the answers yourself.

OR

(2) Describe a problem situation or two involving this issue in communication. Ask how they would handle it, and summarize their answers.

(3) If possible, ask for feedback on your behavior related to this issue.

(4) Look over what you obtained from the items given, and write a brief summary of what you learned through this investigation.

g) Select a work of fiction (novel, short story, play, film) in which there is a relationship between two people which reminds you of one in class or in your everyday life.

(1) Describe the fictional relationship.

(2) Describe the real relationship.

(3) Explore similarities and the implications which the fictional account has for the real relationship, and vice versa, e.g., how could the problems in each be better handled?

(4) Xerox and turn in a key scene which epitomizes the relationship.

h) Carry out a creative project related to some aspect of this course. Two possible approaches are described as follows:

(1) Many important messages about human behavior have been expressed via means other than language. If nonverbal expression is meaningful, you might want to represent in drawings, dance, photographs, collage, sculpture, music or other nonverbal medium some insight or feeling about human relations. Include a brief statement describing your intentions for this project.

(2) Creative writing often can bring out and clarify many inner feelings and motivations. If you would like to try this, write a short story or play, possibly including yourself as the central character, in which some issue related to this course is part of the situation. It might depict a situation very much like one you have experienced, or it might be an imaginary or ideal situation you would someday like to see occur.

i) Write an outline demonstrating how this course might be better taught. Include specific details about the in-and-out-of-class procedures to be used and your rationale for each.

From assignments such as those suggested, students can select one or two to obtain a B and an additional one or two for an A. Or, some could be designated as only B assignments and others as A assignments. Only a few of these options could be offered, thereby limiting student choice; or more could be devised and added to the list, thereby further expanding the available options. The overall objective that I keep in mind is to provide as many options as possible thereby allowing for individual differences in learning needs and styles. All options, however, must be ones that almost inevitably result in worthwhile learning for anyone who undertakes them conscientiously, and must involve a comparable investment of time and energy. Underlying the effort to provide many options is the assumption that when faced with a choice among equally difficult tasks, the student will select the one from which he or she will learn most and, therefore, pursue it wholeheartedly.

4. Despite all efforts to create enjoyable, clearly worthwhile experiences, some safeguards need to be built into the system to discourage procrastination and inadequate effort.

Example: Some of the restrictions I have found necessary are the following:

a) A means for "quality control"—a statement, such as the following, communicates this to students:

There will be one external check on the quality of your work. Every assignment will be read carefully by me and those required for a B or an A will be returned to you marked "satisfactory" or "unsatisfactory." If I feel it is unsatisfactory (which should be rarely), I will add a suggestion which is clear

51

and concrete regarding some additional work needed to bring it up to par. You should have no trouble understanding and doing whatever is necessary to resubmit it in satisfactory form. Once you have completed satisfactory work for the grade you want, you will receive that grade with no further out-of-class work required.

b) Due dates, scattered throughout the semester, are needed to prevent all the work from being put off until the end. For assignments such as these to be meaningful, they must be done in a reasonably unhurried, thoughtful way. When crowded in at the end of the semester, they can easily degenerate into mere busywork.

I have found that enforcing such regulations as attendance requirements and due dates can be unpleasant and difficult. I always seem to relent when excuses are presented. Therefore, I have devised a rather mechanical method of enforcement that allows for some flexibility but also sets clear limits and penalties. This is presented to the students as follows:

If you accumulate 10 penalty points you will be dropped one grade. Three points will be given for each absence and one point for every day an assignment is turned in late. No exceptions to this rule will be made.

With these limitations, students then can receive the grade which they desire at the end of the semester as long as they complete *satisfactorily* the work required (and do not accumulate too many penalty points).

5. The rationale behind providing alternate routes to fulfilling course requirements is twofold:

a) This discipline is more an art than a science. Although there may be only one way to explain a phenomenon of mathematics or chemistry, many kinds of explanations can legitimately be applied to a communication experience. Thus, many approaches are beneficial for studying them.

b) A meta-goal of training in this discipline is to develop students' ability to continue learning on their own. Providing choices and allowing for decisions in academic work is a necessary part of preparation for subsequent self-directed learning, i.e., people learn to be free, self-determining individuals by trying on that posture as students, not by being regimented in behavior at this stage.

Example: Besides allowing for choice-making among a series of teacher-devised approaches to learning, students can be invited to create their own. I usually add the following statement to most course contracts:

I have tried to suggest some assignments that best suit my knowledge about ways people learn most effectively to improve their communication ability. Although this represents the best plan that I can devise at this point for your learning, it is by no means rigid. At all times during the term two invitations are extended to you. First, feel free to discuss with me the rationale for whatever we do, and to question, challenge, or suggest alternatives for anything. Second, if your own interests or needs seem to point you toward some work that does not fit the plan described, another design for learning to improve your communication ability may well be substituted as long as we both agree on its worth.

Providing this final, open-ended option eliminates the mechanistic feeling created at times by some of the contract's structure, for it says that it can all be avoided if the student is willing to determine his or her own approach to learning. It is a testimonial to the intrinsic interest level of the contract that this option is rarely chosen. It is consistent with the philosophy of this whole approach, however, to strongly encourage students to take advantage of this option and to devise activities particularly suited to them.

The contract plan, as suggested in this chapter fulfills the teacher's responsibility to think through the objectives and procedures of the course. It should not, however, eliminate the students' opportunity to do so. The option allowing students to create their own learning plans permits those individuals with special needs or interests to devise an approach ideally suited to them. In essence, this clause in the contract affirms that students can do *whatever* they believe is most worthwhile for them. The only alternative excluded is to do nothing at all, for only an *equivalent* set of assignments will be substituted for those in the contract.

V

In summary, I have advocated here an approach to setting and evaluating experiential objectives for instruction in interpersonal communication. Due to the unique attitudes, ideas, and behavioral patterns which each student develops over the course of a lifetime and brings to classroom study, as well as the differentiation among the contexts in which each plans to use what is learned, uniform objectives for an entire class are inappropriate. Instead, individuals must set and pursue their own objectives. For learning to be applied usefully in the give-and-take of everyday discourse, it must be deeply internalized. This kind of learning cannot be passive. An active, experiential approach to instruction is advised.

First, experiential goals must be established and activities related to each should be devised. These must be experienced without inhibitions created by the fear of being evaluated or graded. Since grading is an unavoidable reality in contemporary educational institutions, a system for grading that is individualized, experiential, and noncompetitive was proposed—a contract. Guidelines and suggestions for creating a contract were offered which have proved valuable to me and my students in the past.

Every instructor, however, needs to devise a course contract suitable for the material he or she will explore, the students in the class, and his or her own beliefs about teaching and learning. It can take many versions and revisions to produce one that yields maximum enthusiasm and learning from one's students and that discriminates those who expend genuinely committed effort from those who do not. When such a contract is developed, however, it becomes an extraordinarily powerful tool for enriching the outcomes of teaching, particularly in interpersonal communication.

Note

In the course of everyday life, one spends much of one's waking hours communicating. Should one wish to improve knowledge and competency in this endeavor, there is no one course in which to learn everything one needs to know and do in order to be optimally effective in the wide range of situations which might be encountered. Consequently, we divide instruction into units that are manageable, areas that can be covered in a semester's time, areas that represent domains of specialty within our field, areas that attend to particular student needs, and areas that circumscribe specific communication variables.

Some of the broadest approaches to division into courses of study of the topics dealt with in our profession are as follows:

a. The nature of the relationship between communicators — e.g., public speaking, interpersonal communication, group dynamics
b. The level or breadth of sophistication with which we will approach the topic — e.g., an introduction to _____ (a broad survey), a special seminar in _____ (a focused examination of a narrow area)
c. The context in which the communication will occur — e.g., business communication, classroom communication, family communication
d. The intent of the communicator — e.g., persuasion, conflict resolution, interviewing
e. The kind of learning that will occur — e.g., theories of _____, research on _____, skill development in _____, case study in _____
f. The people doing the communicating — e.g., women, ethnic minorities, children, the aged, people from other cultures.

Interpersonal communication, therefore, is a multifaceted area which can be approached in many ways. The way we choose to subdivide it affects the nature of the instructional experience. Some methods provide convenient entree to academic literature, since the variables examined are those that have stimulated a clearly defined line of research. Other methods provide a direct link with specific day-to-day situations, since they focus on "how-to's" for people or contexts with which students regularly deal.

Hence, the way we subdivide our discipline also merits a fresh examination. Such a review can elicit new ways of framing the topics we address, highlight omitted areas, suggest new approaches to instruction. The chapters in this part are intended to accomplish all of these aims.

CHAPTER 4

The A-Group: Processes of Authentic Communication

I

A wide range of approaches exists for addressing the domain of interpersonal communication in an introductory course. One way of viewing this spectrum is to imagine a continuum with the term *behavioral* on one end and *phenomenological* on the other. Approaches closer to the former end generally aim to cover the findings of experimental research studies involving interpersonal communication. Approaches closer to the latter end attempt to generate learnings from personal, subjective experiences of students as they interact in class.

Another relevant continuum would have *structured* on one end and *emergent* on the other. A course emphasizing the former would use approaches such as lectures and structured exercises; its sessions would be highly predictable; its organization would reflect the themes addressed in professional literature; learnings would be uniform and readily testable. A course emphasizing the latter would use an approach resembling an encounter group (for a description of the processes involved in this form, see chapter 8); the content of its sessions would defy prediction; the themes examined would most likely reflect material which people work with as relationships develop greater intimacy; and learnings would vary among individuals and be difficult to evaluate.

Each extreme exists in current course offerings; each has inherent value and weaknesses. Behavioral, structured courses offer objectivity, reliability (they are replicable), and control; they elicit complaints of impersonality, detachment, superficiality. Phenomenological, emergent courses offer involvement, spontaneity, and personal investment; they elicit objections on the grounds of being too volatile (even dangerous), too idiosyncratic, and covering too little material. A course designer in this field is tempted to synthesize the two approaches, thereby reaping the benefits and avoiding the pitfalls of each. Such a synthesis is the intent of the course described in this chapter.

A second motivation lies behind this course development. There exists in schools and in society a growing emphasis on discussions intended for *personal growth* (for further elaboration of this trend see chapter 1). The aim is to apply general insights about human nature to the particular lives of participants and to the ongoing process of the discussion group itself. For several reasons this is not an easy process to carry out. It contrasts sharply with most academic dialogue, which usually is quite *impersonal*. Discussion of issues involving people or topics far distant from one's immediate experience is much less ego-involving. In such discussions, only mental mastery is stressed; personal values and feelings usually are ignored.

Most people are accustomed to being guided by a leader or instructor who has a sense of what the "right" answers are. They are not used to assuming responsibility (except within established friendship cliques) for carrying out their own interaction when *sharing* and *opening-ended problem-solving* are the objectives. Understandably so — although these processes potentially can produce much meaningful learning and warm feelings in a group, they can also be easily corrupted. Reticence, confusion, even embarrassment, can result when people inexperienced and unskillful in the processes of personal interaction come together with little guidance.

The scene referred to here is a leaderless group of three to twelve individuals who have come together for the first time as part of a class or community group. They are seated in a circle. Their aim is to create among themselves discourse that is open and frank, that converges on a common theme, but which must be relevant to each of their personal lives to prove useful. What issues in interpersonal communication would concern them?

Fundamentally, an unusual kind of atmosphere must exist for this group to function successfully. Their dialogue must be *authentic*. In other words, participants must look hard at aspects of their everyday behavior that usually operate outside their awareness, that usually are guided by socially conditioned habit patterns. To examine, to challenge, and perhaps to change these is to take a *risk*. It can mean questioning how they were brought up; it can mean seeing old ways of operating as dysfunctional, uninformed, or even as prejudiced; it can mean admitting past mistakes; it can mean disclosing to the group problems they are now facing; it can mean experimenting with new behaviors that at first seem awkward, unattractive, or out of character. People are likely to resist such self-examination and risk-taking if the atmosphere in the group seems dangerous.

Authentic communication is likely to occur only in a group setting where people feel included and known to one another, where they feel cared for and supported, where they sense mutual openness, where they have some influence or control over what happens, and where their problems are heard and worked with effectively. The second aim of this course is to provide guidelines for achieving these conditions within a group.

II

To meet these criteria, I have developed the concept of an A-group. It is one in which *authentic* communication prevails. In an A-group a constellation of specific conditions must exist to the fullest possible extent. Each is created through the exercise of a set of skills. There seem to be five fundamental conditions, which for mnemonic purposes are each given a title beginning with *A*.

These conditions and their requisite skills apply to *intra*personal as well as to *inter*personal communication. (How I treat and present myself is as significant as how I deal with you.) Hence, the unit describing the development of each condition is divided into two parts. One focuses on *self* and the second focuses on communication with *others*.

In addition, in an attempt to maintain the qualities of an emergent course structure, these conditions are sequenced as they would most likely arise as a newly formed cluster of people moves toward becoming an A-group.

Finally, this course is intended to describe and attempt to improve students' ability to handle the skills needed to develop the conditions for an A-group to exist, as indicated in the following list:

1. *Awareness* is the process by which individuals grow to know with finer accuracy and subtlety what they themselves and others believe, feel, and do.

   a) *Self-awareness* is developed as one clarifies goals and recognizes one's own behavior patterns. These processes are nurtured through introspection (examination of one's past experiences) and values clarification (determining priorities among beliefs and commitments). If an individual understands why he or she is in the group, what he or she commonly feels and does in such a setting, and how these patterns might be changed, then he or she is more likely to engage in productive communication.

   b) *Other-awareness* is developed as one perceives with greater accuracy the people whom one encounters. People are prone to form hasty impressions based more on past experience than on the actual data available. Attraction to others is affected by these impressions. Knowledge of impression formation and interpersonal attraction factors are likely to keep this process more tentative and conscious so that more accurate awareness of one another results. At the beginning of a group, people's "orienting" and "inclusion" needs predominate, i.e., Who are these people? How do I want to be with them? Do they want to be with me? These issues are considered in this unit.

2. *Acceptance* is the degree to which people perceive and express worth in themselves and others.

a) *Self-acceptance* is the trust, the confidence, the OKness one feels about oneself. When one senses one's worth as a unique individual, one is more likely to express oneself freely and to accept others as they are. A positive self-concept leads to greater enjoyment and enthusiastic participation in a group. Reticence, incessant talking, and hyperconforming talk are symptoms of a negative self-concept. Strengthening self-esteem is the aim of this unit.

b) *Other-acceptance* involves psychological tolerance, compassion, and trust for people. It also includes the overt indication of those feelings through expressions of interest, support, and affection. People need clear invitations to share their ideas and validation of the worth of what they have to say. This encouragement and "stroking" are important building blocks for developing the atmosphere in which authentic communication is most likely to occur.

3. *Actualizing* is the spontaneous, open sharing of one's ideas and feelings in the process of moving deeper and closer to others.

a) *Self-actualizing* can be experienced as simply the venting of feelings, catharsis, or "getting things off your chest." It is what occurs as people open up to one another. A second form is self-disclosure, in which people share perceptions and experiences that usually remain hidden due to social norms. These are often the unresolved issues in a person's life or any comment that risks disapproval from others. It is the talk that is clearly more "open and honest" than usual everyday conversation.

b) *Other-actualizing* includes the ways in which we encourage or inhibit others from being fully themselves. Within this section are active listening skills that assure people they are being fully understood and consciousness-raising skills that allow people to express parts of themselves not usually tolerated within their sex, age, ethnic, or professional role. Finally, it includes processes that stimulate creative self-expression in forms such as poetry, art, movement, and music.

4. *Assertion* is the exercise of influence or control over one's own behavior or the overall situation in which one finds himself or herself. It is a display of strength or certainty when something of personal significance merits expression.

a) *Self-asserting* behavior articulates one's own rights without violating those of others. Standing up for a belief or for the right of self-determination belongs here. The ability to avoid behavior perceived as aggressive or imposing is essential, as well as whatever would underplay one's own point of view in a too-placating manner.

b) *Other-asserting* behavior involves responding to conflict situations created by someone else, dealing with confrontation, anger, criticism. Fights between people who must live or work closely together are virtually inevitable. However, if they are handled openly and fairly they can lead to deeper levels of trust, understanding, and mutual satisfaction. There are several ways of approaching such experiences, a mastery of which can help significantly in optimizing positive outcomes.

5. *Aid* is the process whereby a personal problem is examined and worked through to a satisfying resolution. It occurs when one notes a disturbing discrepancy between how things are and how they might preferably be.

a) *Self-aiding* is what one can do to help oneself. It can start with clarification of the problem situation, progress through expression of the feelings created, move to a deeper understanding of the current state of affairs versus how things need to change, and culminate in the development and implementation of a plan to create that change. One can learn to think through a situation more clearly, to affect one's own mind-body state, and to carry out a plan for self-modification of behavior — thereby gaining a deeper sense of personal power and responsibility for one's thinking, feeling, and behaving.

b) *Other-aiding* is the process whereby one helps another to work through the steps just outlined. Here it is essential to communicate the unconditional regard, empathy, and genuineness necessary to be seen as a trustworthy partner in this endeavor. Once such rapport is developed, the helper functions as a consultant who assists the other to work through a series of problem-solving steps toward the resolution that best suits him/her.

III

The rationale, aims, and topics for a course on authentic communication have been summarized. The next concern is *how* are these to be pursued? Here a contrast must be drawn: ideally, the instructor and a group of twelve students meet as a group to discuss these topics emphasizing their personal applications; realistically, such an approach is impractical. Rarely is such a low teacher-student ratio viable in a school setting.

At the University of Kansas, I teach a course dealing with this material to a group of 100 students each semester. This is done using the synthesis of *behavioral, structured* and *phenomenological, emergent* approaches mentioned earlier. This amalgam includes the following elements:

1. The class meets once a week for a three-hour session in the evening. (This can be divided into three to five hour-long segments when such an arrangement is necessary.)

2. At the first session the overall schema is introduced. Thereafter, one of the ten units is covered at each class session. There is a concluding session at the end.

3. Each session includes two major phases. The first is a lecture reviewing the primary concepts that apply to understanding the session's theme. The second is a small group meeting at which the lecture concepts are discussed and an exercise carried out that focuses students' attention on how the session's theme applies to their own everyday behavior, or to the group itself.

4. For small group meetings the class is divided into groups of about ten students each. These are formed to mix as much as possible men and women, and people of different ages, majors, and experience, in group interaction. People who already know each other are separated, so that everyone begins as strangers. Thus, among themselves they will experience from "scratch" the development of an A-group with a rich variety of individuals.

5. These groups remain intact throughout the semester, thereby allowing the necessary time and contact for growth toward authentic communication. Sitting in with each group are two student leaders. They are volunteers from a previous semester's class who performed unusually well in their own group. They have taken other courses in interpersonal communication, and usually intend to enter a career that involves working with groups of people.

6. Prior to each class session I meet for an hour with the group leaders. We review the previous week's session; we discuss problem group members or situations that they found difficult to handle; we preview the content of the upcoming lecture; and we discuss alternative exercises to be employed during the group meeting. The alternatives are described in terms of the group climate to which they are best suited, i.e., "This one is most apt if your group is comfortable and open to sharing"; "This one should be used if they still are wary and inhibited."

7. The responsibilities of group leaders are spelled out in a brief contract, a summary of which follows.

    The role of group leader has two primary functions. These are to help your group members to have as rich a learning experience as possible and to provide an opportunity for you to practice using your own human relations skills in the capacity of leader. In order to carry out these functions optimally, you will be expected to do several things.

a) We will meet for one hour each week to review what has been happening in each group and to prepare for the upcoming class session.

b) We will meet for a conference about the fourth week of the semester to discuss how your group is doing and your comments on papers.

c) You will meet with your groups weekly, and your role will include the following responsibilities:
   (1) Getting the people together and starting the session
   (2) Leading a brief discussion on the lecture and any other concerns that might exist
   (3) Introducing and leading a brief sharing of responses to the "Preview Question" for the week
   (4) Introducing and leading the exercise
   (5) Introducing and leading a brief closing "go-round" in which the group summarizes what they have learned during that session
   (6) Collecting and returning students' papers
   (7) Collecting feedback on the session.

d) You will read and write comments on the papers of the people in your group that include:
   (1) Praise for particularly insightful or well-written passages
   (2) Questions about areas they seem to have omitted
   (3) Suggestions for issues they might consider
   (4) References to comparable experiences that you have had
   (5) Requests for them to bring things up in the group
   (6) Requests for them to apply their ideas more to themselves or to the group
   (7) Support when they touch on a personally vulnerable area.

e) You will meet with each member of your group at least once during the semester for a conference to:
   (1) Reaffirm your interest in their paper material
   (2) Encourage them to do better (or do as well as they have done) in the group
   (3) Elicit concerns they hesitate to bring up in the group
   (4) Share with them your feelings about the group.

f) You will keep records on your group members' attendance, submission of papers, participation, and paper grades.

g) You will turn in to me, on the fourth, seventh, tenth, and thirteenth week of the semester a brief statement (one or two pages) answering these questions:
   (1) What aspects of your group are going well?

63

(2) What aspects of your group need improvement?

(3) How might I improve the preceding three weeks' group sessions in future classes?

(4) How might I improve the upcoming group sessions?

(5) How are you working with your partner?

(6) How might we improve our group leaders' meetings?

(7) What is your assessment of the students' written work?

8. For each class session besides the group meetings, a second device is employed to encourage each student to apply the concepts introduced. This is a structured outside meeting held during the ensuing week with another member of the group. This dyadic encounter permits a more intense, involving communication challenge (for an explanation of the rationale underlying the use of dyads see chapter 9) and promotes a deeper level of mutual acquaintanceship among group members.

9. After each class session, students must complete a weekly *reaction report*. This report includes four sections:

a) *Lecture review question* which demands that students apply concepts introduced in the lecture to specific personal situations

b) *Group review question* whose purpose is to encourage understanding how to learn from interaction in which they have participated, i.e., they are to identify a personally relevant experience in the group meeting and to develop a general principle about their own communication from it

c) *Dyad review question* whose purpose is similar, i.e., to extract from the dyad experience a meaningful concept about that week's A-group theme

d) *Preview question* whose purpose is to encourage preliminary thinking about the upcoming week's theme, thereby preparing students to gain more from that session. This usually is done by asking for recall of a past experience in which that theme played an important part.

10. In addition to these reaction reports students need to read text material and carry out individualized learning projects. (The approach to developing these projects is described in chapter 3, as is the method for determining the course grade).

IV

Space does not permit providing an outline of the lecture material covered in each session. However, this section provides some group exercises, as well as dyadic activities and reaction report questions that are included in this course. In practice, these are supplemented by oral instructions; they are presented here only in skeletal form. Hopefully, they are complete enough for the experienced reader to visualize.

Introduction

Lecture Review Question

We talked in class about the meaning of "personal growth." Try to recall one experience you have had in a relationship with someone else that had the effect of stimulating you to grow in any of the ways discussed. Describe first what happened, and then add, "The moral of this story is___" and try to come up with a principle about relating to people that still affects your life today.

Dyad Activity

The purpose is to get to know the personal patterns of someone in your group better, to share your own, and to explore your first impressions.

Before meeting with your partner, circle the item from each pair given that is most like you. When you get together share your answers. First, however, try to guess what your partner circled before he or she tells you. This will tell each of you how accurate your first impressions are before you get to know each other.

Feel free to discuss what needs, values, or habits underlie the choices each of you made (as well as what you think each term refers to). Also, try to share the cues on which you based your first impressions.

    Are you: More of a saver than a spender?
              More of a loner than a grouper?
              More like Kansas or Colorado?
              More yes than no?
              More here than there?
              More political than apolitical?
              More like the country than the city?
              More of a leader than a follower?
              More physical than mental?
              More establishment than antiestablishment?
              More like a tortoise or a hare?
              More like an electric typewriter or a quill pen?
              More like a clothesline or a kite string?
              More like a flyswatter or flypaper?
              More like a file cabinet or a liquor cabinet?
              More like a bubbling brook or a placid lake?

Dyad Review Question

Afterward, write a paragraph or two regarding the major similarities and differences between you and the other person, how your impressions of the person compared with how he or she actually was, how you felt about this dyadic experience, and one "lesson" or general principle that might explain what occurred.

We will be working next week on self-awareness. There are many sides to the "self." One is the "ideal self," or how you would like to be. Another is the "real self," or how you see yourself now. Write a paragraph contrasting where you are now and how you ideally would like to grow in regard to human relations.

There is no group meeting for the first session.

Self-Awareness

Lecture Review Question

We talked about the role of self-awareness in human relations and about ways of improving it. Drawing upon this material, respond to these two problem situations:

  a. A friend who is considering breaking up with a longtime dating partner asks you to help him or her think through this decision. What questions might you ask?
  b. Another friend who is trying to pick a field in which to major also asks your help in making this decision. What questions would you ask in this situation?

Group Review Question

What was the effect on your group and yourself of people sharing their self-awareness in response to the questions? What does this suggest about the process of becoming acquainted outside the group?

Dyad Activity

The purpose is to focus on and share self-awareness and to note the effect. This week when you meet in dyads, do not spend the time exchanging comments. Instead, for half of the time (about 20 minutes) one person will be the speaker and the other will listen. The listener can ask questions, but essentially attention will be focused on one person at a time — the speaker. After 20 minutes are up, switch roles, and for the second half hour the listener will become the speaker.

During each person's speaking time, he or she is to tell the other his or her life story in terms of one or more aspects of human relations. You might talk about the friends you've had since you were a child or about your family, about your experiences in school or in your hometown, about your experiences with shyness or with being assertive, etc. If you'd like, you can just review your human relations history in general. If you complete telling about one issue, then switch to another until the 20 minutes are up.

Dyad Review Question

Write a paragraph describing your experience as speaker and as listener. Compare the experiences in terms of the content shared and how each of you talked. Develop one general principle about what usually occurs when you share at such length about yourself.

Preview Question

Think of someone with whom you generally enjoy spending time and someone you would rather avoid. Try to recall the first time you met each person. Were you able then to predict what your future relationship with each would be? What specific clues can you recall using to form your first impressions of these people?

Group Exercise

The purposes of this exercise are to develop self-awareness of what people want to know about each other when they begin to interact and to start the process whereby they share their self-awareness and begin getting to know each other. Ask participants to think of the one question they most would like others to answer (and that they would be willing to answer themselves). Questions should be written anonymously on slips of paper that are folded and placed in the center of the group. One paper is then picked out and read aloud; each person is invited to offer a response or to pass. Continue discussing each question until all are covered or time runs out.

Other-Awareness

Lecture Review Question

We talked about several factors that seem to explain why people are attracted to one another. Consider these forces in regard to at least two people in your group. What attraction forces lead you to want to get to know them better?

Group Review Question

What did you learn from their guesses about how people in your group see you? What did you learn about the categories you use in forming impressions from the errors you made in guessing others' responses?

Dyad Activity

Meet with your partner in a place where one of you knows several people, e.g., in a class, at a familiar bar or restaurant, or anywhere else that you are likely to see your acquaintances. The "stranger" should share with the "native" his or her first impressions of the people you see. Try to be as specific as possible about the particular cues used to develop inferences about the people observed. Be as open as you can about what you think each person is like from his or her appearance or behavior. You might need to discuss whether the native would feel hurt if the impressions were negative. Try to understand *why* you are making those assumptions (e.g., the person reminds you of someone else).

The native should give his opinion of how accurate the impressions are, based on having more experience with the individuals being observed. He or she might point out specific aspects that are overlooked or misunderstood by the stranger, as well as noting when the impressions are on target.

If possible, go to a spot where the roles can be reversed, so that each can have a comparable experience.

Dyad Review Question

Comment on this dyad by summarizing what the experience was like and by noting what you learned about how you and/or your partner form impressions and how accurate they are.

Preview Question

Try to recall an experience in which you got to know someone better through an experience that involved much more than words, i.e., your nonverbal communication. Examples might be working together, playing a game, touching, or any activity wherein the other person revealed himself or herself as much or more through what he/she *did* than through what was said.

Group Exercises

    a. Remind the group that they all had first impressions of one another that may or may not have changed. Suggest that volunteers ask the group: *What were your first impressions of me and how have they changed?* Refer their thinking to what their impressions say about *themselves.*

or

    b. This exercise involves several steps:

        1) Ask participants to tear a sheet of paper into fourths.

        2) Distribute the following sheet and ask them to insert names of group members.

        3) Ask them to answer the first question on one of their small sheets.

        4) Collect these sheets and number them.

        5) Read each aloud. Ask them to guess who wrote it and to put that number in a box next to the person's name.

        6) Reread each aloud and ask them to identify the one they wrote, while each person checks his/her accuracy (by circling correct guesses).

        7) Discuss the reasons for right and wrong guesses.

        8) Repeat process for second question, etc., using a different reader each time.

HOW ACCURATELY DO YOU READ PEOPLE?

1. Something about me that most people use to form their impression of me is _____.

2. A belief that I might risk my life for is _____.

3. A person in some way unlike me in this group is _____. A person in some way very much like me in this group is _____.

4. Usually, only people who know me for a while are aware that I _____.

NAMES	1	2	3	4
1.				
2.				
3.				
4.				
5.				
6.				
7.				
8.				
9.				
10.				
11.				
12.				

Other-Awareness II: Body Language

Lecture Review Question

We discussed several aspects of nonverbal communication. Select any one of these cues and recall one instance in your *group* and one instance in your *everyday life* when it played a crucial role in determining how you reacted to someone, or how someone may have reacted to you. Describe each situation and the nonverbal cue to which you or the other person reacted most strongly.

Group Review Question

Describe your group's activity last week and develop a general principle of what happens in you *or* among people when nonverbal communication is emphasized.

Dyad Activity

We can tune into the nonverbal dimension most effectively when we ourselves are silent. Therefore, begin your dyad this week by becoming acquainted (the better you know the person, the easier this dyad will be) and then decide upon any activity you can do together for about half an hour that does not require speaking. I suggest going for a walk through a natural setting and perhaps through several places where people are gathered. Just look around you, touch things, listen to the sounds in each area, even taste and smell whatever you can. Communicate with each other by using nonverbal signs and signals whenever you can. You might take turns being leader on your trek or walking while one person's eyes are closed and the other guides him or her around. Observe people and animals; interact with them. See what is available when words don't get in the way. Spend your last few minutes together talking over your experience.

Dyad Review Question

During a time when words are not used attention is given more to other things inside oneself and in the environment. What did you do during this period of enforced silence and how did it affect your awareness?

Preview Question

Our session next week will deal with self-acceptance. To think about it in advance, identify one aspect about yourself that you do *not* feel good about and consider how that judgment has affected your way of relating with other people, *or* answer this question in regard to someone else whom you know well.

Group Exercises

    a. Participants gave each other feedback verbally last week. This week they might want to try it nonverbally. Ask someone to volunteer to move into the center of the group, then ask others to go up to him or her and express a message of any kind nonverbally. Person in center might have eyes closed. Ask that person to tell how he or she reacted to these messages and clear up any misunderstandings.

    b. Ask people in the group to go, one at a time, into the center of the group and to combine themselves, without speaking, into a sculpture or tableau that represents the group and the various interpersonal relationships that exist. Use the dimensions of space, posture, etc., to convey meaning. Or ask for a volunteer to move people into that person's vision of how things are.

    c. Ask participants to spend one minute with each person in the group, in dyads, having a nonverbal conversation. You announce when the minute is up and they must move on.

d. Discuss how nonverbal cues have affected interaction in this group, especially inclusion, affection, and control.
e. Play a game of charades. Each person starts by tearing a piece of paper in fourths and then writing a sentence on each piece of at least *five* words that is about the *self* using one of the *feeling words* introduced in the class exercise. Then divide the group in half. One person from each group alternates taking turns. That person shuffles his/her other papers and then picks one to be acted out. He or she does it and is timed. Allow for feedback between each segment. The group with the lowest total time wins.
f. Divide the group into pairs and ask each to think of an incident in which two people are talking but not saying all that they really feel. Ask them to role-play their incident for the others who will try to guess what is unspoken from nonverbal cues. (This is charades in reverse. The actors are trying to hide their true feelings.)
g. A part of nonverbal awareness is the images people evoke in others' minds. A way to deal with these is to play the game, "Metaphors." One person closes his or her eyes. The others pick someone to describe. The first person then asks everyone, "If this person were a _____ what would he/she be?" From these metaphors (such as animal, plant, movie star, article of clothing, part of the body, TV show, etc.) the person with eyes closed tries to guess who has been picked. Remember to encourage people to explain *why* they selected their particular answer.

Self-Acceptance

Lecture Review Question

We discussed the effects of a lack of self-acceptance on a person's manner of communication. Several dysfunctional communication styles are listed. Discuss how there could be a connection between any *three* of them and a lack of self-acceptance:

a. Someone who is shy, quiet, reserved
b. Someone who talks incessantly, who goes on and on connecting one idea to another in an endless string
c. Someone who is always joking, entertaining, amusing others
d. Someone who is cool, tough, hard-nosed, the strong silent type

Group Review Question

The group session called for you to identify and affirm parts of yourself. Some people find it easier to accept others than to affirm themselves; with others the opposite is true. Did you find yourself liking others' drawings more readily than your own? the same? or less? How is this pattern of judging reflected in your life and relationships in general?

Dyad Activity

The dyad activity this week calls for each of you to affirm and share something about yourself. Give some thought beforehand to the things you are interested in. These might include an activity, a skill, a person, something you've done, something in your home, your field of study, your religion, an author you enjoy reading, a place you have visited, etc. When you get together discuss your lists, and each pick the one thing from the other person's options that you would most like to learn about. Allow 15–20 minutes for the first person to be an expert and the other to be a learner. The point is to take time to experience having something about yourself that is worthwhile to share. Next, switch roles. Finally, be sure to discuss the feelings that arose as you thought about what to share and as you experienced each role in the lesson.

Dyad Review Question

Being an "expert" or a "teacher" can be uncomfortable at first for someone who most often has been in the learner's role. What did you share in this dyad and how did each role feel to you, at the beginning, and then after you got into it?

Preview Question

List what you believe are three of your personal strengths in human relations (e.g., good listener, assertive, warm, loyal, etc.).

To understand the effect of others' reactions on your self-concept, try to recall for each of them a time when someone praised or affirmed you for that characteristic.

Group Exercises

a. Ask each person to look back at the lifeline drawn earlier this semester and to take no more than five minutes to share with the group a description of the times when he or she felt most proud of themselves and most glad to be alive during each segment of their lives. (You can add ashamed, bad, embarrassed, if you think this is one-sided.)

    Allow a little time for discussion between each statement.

b. Distribute the following sheet and ask each person to follow its instructions.

This task includes several steps calling for you to express yourself creatively and then to share and synthesize what you do with the others in your group.

1) Write the question, "Who am I?" on the back of this sheet. Then answer it by creating a list of about six or seven words or phrases that describe you most appropriately. (This was done once before during our session on self-awareness.)

2) For each word on your list, spontaneously create a drawing that somehow symbolically represents that aspect of your being. (Since you're drawing parts of yourself, there is no "good" or "bad" label that can be put on these by anyone else. So draw as freely as you like.)

3) Look over the series of drawings you have just made. Now create one additional drawing that synthesizes these aspects, that shows how they interact to form the whole being that you are.

4) Join with someone else in your group and share with that person your separate drawings and the one in which you synthesized them. Discuss what each means, if you wish. (You might ask your partner to guess at the meaning before telling him/her.) Use the drawings to get to know each other better.

5) With this partner create a "Who are we?" drawing in which you symbolically represent how your two individual beings interrelate. (You can discuss this before beginning to draw, or just start with a clean sheet of paper and draw simultaneously, seeing what happens as you go along.)

6) Meet with your whole group, having each person share something about what each one drew about him/herself and the drawing made with a partner.

7) As a group create a drawing that expresses how all of your individualities blend into a group and/or a drawing that represents your group as an organism with an identity of its own.

8) Discuss the process you underwent in creating the group drawing together.

Other-Acceptance

We discussed the role and forms of support in human relations. Apply what you heard in class in commenting upon three of the situations mentioned.

    a. A boss withholds praise for employees stating, "They'll work harder if they're trying to prove themselves than if they're confident."

    b. A parent withholds praise from a child stating, "I don't want my child to get a swelled head."

    c. An athlete is being praised by a sportscaster, and responds, "Aw, shucks, it was nothing."

    d. Someone gives this feedback to a friend, "You shouldn't be so positive and supportive all the time. People don't really believe you."

Group Review Question

We discussed the human need for validation and common inhibitions about giving it freely. Summarize what you did in your group, how freely support was given, and the effect on the group of exchanging or withholding it.

Dyad Activity

It is often hard for some people to reveal openly their strengths and achievements. However, this capacity can be very important for future personal and professional success. This dyad experience is intended to provide an opportunity to explore this kind of interaction.

After getting to know each other, divide your time in half. First, one person is an "eliciter" and the other is a "responder." The goal of the eliciter is to encourage his or her partner to talk about strengths and positive abilities.

This might be done by asking some of these questions:

    a. Recalling the lifeline you drew in an earlier class: What were the times when you felt most proud of yourself, when you did something well, or just felt good to be alive during the years you were in elementary school? when you were in junior high? high school? college? during vacations? at jobs you have had? at home?

    b. What do you consider your personal qualities, talents, skills, etc.?

    c. When has someone validated you? When have you validated someone else? When have you wanted to validate someone, but couldn't do so fully? When have you felt uncomfortable about praise given you?

    d. What are your hopes, dreams, ambitions for the future in regard to a job or career? in regard to a service to your community, nation, or mankind? in regard to your home or family life?

After one person has interviewed the other for about twenty minutes, switch roles. Afterward, discuss how it felt to emphasize the positive so intensely.

Dyad Review Question

Summarize what your experience in this dyad was like and suggest one general principle about how people respond to being encouraged to validate themselves.

Preview Question

Some people say it is better to be an "open book," to show yourself fully to people. Others say it is better to "keep them guessing," to reveal very little about yourself. Try to recall and describe a situation from your life in which one or the other of these positions seemed to hold true, when it was clearly to your benefit to be open and honest *or* when it was best to keep something to yourself.

a. This exercise will provide an opportunity for students to give and receive positive feedback. It includes these steps:
   1) List, as a group, a number of communication qualities or strengths that might have positive value at some point in a group like yours.
   2) Ask each person which he or she finds more difficult, validating or affirming others or being validated.
   3) Depending on each person's choice, the task is either to give positive feedback to every person in the group or to ask each person, "What is a strength or potential that you see me as having?"
   4) Discuss how the target person felt about his or her experience and then what others perceived as the person was involved in the experience.

b. A milder form of this exercise is to remind students that support can be a significant gift to provide another person. Ask them to exchange such gifts by writing a brief note to each person in the group pointing out a positive attribute they have noticed in the course of the past few weeks together, or on a dyad. Suggest that they try to recall something not blatantly obvious. These notes are then exchanged and their content can be shared and/or discussed by anyone who chooses to do so.

Self-Actualizing

Lecture Review Question

We talked about the risks and benefits of self-actualizing or personal sharing. Imagine that the following situations were to arise, what would you ask and/or advise each person:

a. A friend wants to know if he or she should discuss use of marijuana with parents.
b. A friend asks what he or she should do about knowing that several classmates are conspiring to cheat on an upcoming test.
c. Another member of your group asks whether to discuss his or her current problems with a girl or boy friend with the group.

Group Review Question

You experimented with self-disclosure in the current group activity. From what you did or observed, develop a general principle as to when it is (or isn't) appropriate to risk self-disclosure.

Dyad Activity

It is interesting and insightful to identify the aspects of self that are easy to share and aspects that you prefer to keep private. It can also be valuable to experience trying to expand your limits by being more open.

To do so, begin by rating the items listed: put an "E" next to those areas that you would find "easy" to talk about; put an "H" next to those that are "harder" to share; put an "S" next to really "sensitive" areas. Then, meet with your partner.

One person picks an E area and shares how it is dealt with in his or her own life (not about the topic in general). The other person then offers his or her perspective. Next, it is the second person's turn to pick an area to talk about, after which the first person responds. Alternate this way until the E's have been exhausted, and proceed as far through the H's and S's as you wish or time permits.

Neither of you should feel pressured to reveal anything you don't want to. Probing questions by the listener are OK, but "I'd rather not say any more about that" is always an appropriate answer. Of course, you should agree to keep your conversation confidential.

a. My hobbies, interests, and favorite leisure pursuits.
b. What I like and dislike about my body—appearance, health, etc.
c. My school and outside work—satisfactions, frustrations.
d. My financial situation: income, savings, debts, investments, etc.
e. Aspects of my parents I like and dislike; family problems encountered in growing up.
f. Religious views, philosophy of life, what gives meaning to my life.
g. My love life, past and present.
h. My political views and practices.
i. Problems in my marriage, or in my dealings with opposite sex at present.
j. My use and views of drugs and alcohol.
k. What I like, dislike about my partner, on the basis of this encounter.

Dyad Review Question

How did what happened in this dyad compare with what you had expected beforehand? What factors in your dialogue affected what occurred?

Preview Question

There are people with whom we feel free to be fully overselves and people with whom we sense a need to be somewhat reserved, play a role, show only a part of ourselves. Picture an individual you know in each of these categories and try to describe each, emphasizing what they do that allows you to be fully or only partially self-actualizing.

Group Exercises

a. Each person writes on a sheet of paper, anonymously, something about self that he or she would hesitate to tell most people or this group. These sheets are folded and put in a pile in the middle of the group. One is chosen and read aloud. People discuss how they would react to hearing it and how it applies to their own lives. The writer is identified only if he or she wishes.
b. Ask each person to recall one feeling experienced but withheld in the group. Ask for a volunteer to share such a feeling. First, ask others to observe the volunteer for conformity to approach suggested in the lecture. After sharing, a target person must paraphrase what was heard until the speaker is satisfied that he or she was understood. Ask that they continue this exchange until each is satisfied that it is complete. Ask each one to react to what they did, then ask for observers' reactions, before moving on to the next exchange.
c. Distribute the following sheet and ask each person to follow directions.

People often avoid expressing feelings toward others for fear of being misunderstood, obligating the other person to respond, or becoming too vulnerable. Repressing feelings can be damaging to oneself and to relationships. Overdoing the expression of feelings, however, also can be inappropriate. In this exercise we will practice avoiding these dangers by owning, specifying, and targeting feelings, as well as by inviting feedback about them.

1) List the names of several people with whom you interact regularly in the left-hand column.

2) Check the feelings that person arouses in you (in the right-hand column).
3) Circle the checks that refer to feelings you express *less* fully than you really experience. Also, circle any that you overdo.
4) Pick one of these areas to work on now.
5) Think of an incident that might come up in the future in which this feeling would arise.
6) Ask someone to role-play the person saying or doing what would trigger your feeling.
7) This is done three times, while you:
   (a) Repress or avoid expressing your feelings
   (b) Overdo or exaggerate your feelings
   (c) Express your feelings appropriately, as was suggested in class.
8) Discuss observers' comments on your responses, how you felt in each response position, and how the role-player felt as a result of each response.

NAMES	caring warmth love	resent- ment anger	disappoint- ment hurt	anxiety fear	with- drawal boredom
1.					
2.					
3.					
4.					
5.					

Other-Actualizing

Lecture Review Question

We discussed some of the characteristics of a dialogue among people that produces personal growth. This kind of talk can be very intense; it can also be dangerous if mishandled. Considering the pros and cons of such an encounter, discuss your beliefs about three of the following concepts:

a. Honesty is always the best policy.
b. Only your best friend will tell you _____.
c. Love means never having to say you're sorry.
d. Behold the turtle, the only way he makes progress is to stick his neck out.
e. It is better to be safe than sorry.

Group Review Question

The group session called for you to receive concentrated attention from others. Consider if and why it was stimulating or oppressive to be on the spot like that.

Dyad Question

Feelings can be such potent experiences that people hesitate to talk about them openly. Consequently, we can come to believe that our emotional experiences are unique. We will be working against this tendency in the dyads this week.

Share with your partner some of your most memorable experiences involving strong feelings. You might begin by picking any of the situations suggested here and exchanging a recollection each of you has about it. Talk about as many as you wish or time permits.

Keep in mind that the job of the listener is simply to hear and understand what is being told — *not* to try to interpret, analyze, probe, advise, moralize, or in any way act as counselor or judge.

a. A time when you felt especially angry at someone
b. A time when you felt especially tense, nervous, or scared
c. A time when you felt most happy, joyful, glad to be alive
d. A time when you felt really cared for, loved, or when you felt this way about someone else
e. A time when you felt badly disappointed, hurt, grief, or pain.

Dyad Review Question

After discussing past emotional experiences, did you feel more similar to or more different from your partner? Why do you think this is so?

Preview Question

We will be discussing self-assertion at our next session. To begin thinking about this process, recall and describe briefly two instances: one in which you wanted to ask for or affirm something but withheld the statement, and another in which you risked speaking up for what you wanted or believed in.

Group Exercises

a. Personal sharing helps people to get to know one another better. Ask people who want to be known better by the group to volunteer to be asked questions by others. The volunteer says, "I would like you to know me better, so you are welcome to ask me any question you would like." The volunteer is free to refuse or partially answer any question. The questioner can stop the volunteer at any time by saying, "Thank you." (He or she should also say this after every answer.) Each person in the group gets to ask one question or pass.

Sample questions:

1) Would you name three people you admire?
2) When was a time that you felt really proud of yourself?
3) What one thing would you like to change about yourself?
4) What do you think you will be doing in three years?
5) What is your earliest memory?
6) What are your religious beliefs?
7) For whom, if anyone, will you vote in the election?
8) How do you feel about this group?
9) How do you feel about me?
10) How do you feel about being asked these questions?

b. Exercise "a" from the preceding Group Exercises.

Self-Assertion

Lecture Review Question

We discussed several areas where people might be more assertive and methods of practicing this behavior effectively. To apply these concepts to your own life, identify one right that you have denied yourself and do the following:

a. Describe a situation in which this issue might arise again in the future, including the time, place, and people involved, as well as the right in question.

b. Write a passive response you might make.

c. Write an aggressive response you might make.

d. Write two assertive responses you might make.

Group Review Question

You discussed and experimented with assertiveness in the group. Summarize what you did and the effect this topic had on your *group* and on how *you* see the others.

Dyad Activity

You are welcome to do any of the following activities:

a. Discuss current conflict situations in your past and/or present lives.

b. Get a copy of today's newspaper and go through it slowly, page by page, from front to back. Whenever either of you sees an article or an advertisement about which you have an opinion, stop and share it (e.g., what the President should do on a given question, welfare is given too freely, women's fashions today are ridiculous, basketball is overemphasized, etc.). The other person should then give an opinion; if a conflict exists you can pursue the issue with a discussion if you wish. Of course, discussions are encouraged. Afterward, discuss the kind of assertiveness each of you used.

c. Discuss the meaning of the following quotations in your own lives:

(1) "Not everything that is faced can be changed, but nothing can be changed until it is faced." — James Baldwin.

(2) "Are you aware that anger is closely linked to love and that you can and usually do get angry at people you love? Love and anger are not mutually exclusive. You can get deeply angry at people and love them enough so that you want the very best of all things for them." — Theodore Issac Rubin.

(3) "Our marriage used to suffer from arguments that were too short. Now we argue long enough to find out what the argument is about." — Hugh Prather.

Dyad Review Question

Based on consideration of yourself in this dyad and, in general, regarding assertiveness, write a brief self-description about how you handle disagreements.

Preview Question

Recall one conflict situation that has come up in your group or outside life (a time when at least two people wanted different things to happen), describe what each person wanted, and how the conflict was resolved.

Group Exercises

a. Have group members role-play responses to situations in their own lives that require assertion.

1) One person describes or demonstrates behavior that he or she wants to respond to assertively.

2) Another group member plays the role, providing the comment to initiate the assertive behavior. This is done three times:

a) The first time the response is passive.

b) The second time the response is aggressive.

c) The third time the response is assertive.

b. Discuss how people's assertive rights have been honored or violated in your group. Provide opportunities for people to respond assertively.

c. It can be helpful to practice dealing with common group problems. Ask which of the people described most irritates group members. Then ask one volunteer to be a confronter and one to be confronted. The confronter picks the problem. The group talks generally about anything and the second volunteer acts out the role. When ready, the first volunteer initiates the confrontation and interaction continues until it is completed or until the assertiveness styles of both participants have been clearly demonstrated.

1) A person who often criticizes the behavior of others

2) A person who is extremely shy and quiet

3) A person who jokes about other people's problems

4) A person is so "nice" that he or she is unreal

5) A person whose only way of helping one with a problem is to go on and on about something similar that happened to him or her

6) A person who comes to class "stoned" every time

Discuss what each participant and the observers felt and how they reacted to the conflict styles.

Other-Assertion

Lecture Review Question

We discussed several methods for dealing with conflict. Each is appropriate under different circumstances. Select one relationship in your life (e.g., with your group, your roommate, your father, your child, etc.) and identify a situation in which it would be best to use each of the approaches listed:

a. accommodating

b. forcing, dominating

c. avoiding

d. compromising or problem-solving

Group Review Question

You may have opened up some areas of potential conflict in the group. Recall what one person did that helped the group to air and consider a conflict and what another did to suppress or distort a conflict.

Dyad Activity

In learning how to handle conflicts constructively, the first step is to become aware of your present and past style of managing conflict. Think back over the interpersonal conflicts you have been involved in during the past few years. These conflicts may be with friends, parents, brothers and sisters, girl friends or boyfriends, husbands or wives, teachers or students, or with your boss or subordinates. In the spaces following, list the three major conflicts you can remember and how you resolved them. Since space is limited, you may wish to abbreviate by writing down only the key words describing your style of conflict management and the conflict situations in which you have been involved.

Each person should begin by filling in the chart which deals with that person's style of conflict management. When completed, spend the rest of the hour sharing what you have written, discussing the situations described (what was effective and what wasn't, how each might have been resolved better, etc.), and exchanging ideas about the difficulties of conflict resolution in general.

My Conflicts   *How I Resolved the Conflict*

_____

_____

_____

Dyad Review Question

You may have found that you and/or your partner deal with conflict in a patterned or consistent way or that you have used a variety of approaches. In either case, identify one general principle about handling conflict that you have learned from this recall and sharing experience that you might apply in the future to improve your effectiveness in a conflict situation.

Preview Question

We will be talking about self-aid next week. By this we mean that people can help themselves to move from one emotional state to another. Recall what you have done for yourself at some time in the past to relieve or deal with any two of the following feelings: (a) anger, (b) depression, (c) disappointment, (d) anxiety, fear, (e) grief, (f) jealousy, (g) embarrassment, (h) loneliness, (i) shock, (j) frustration, (k) guilt, (l) pressure.

Group Exercises

    a. This exercise provides feedback on conflicts between self-concept and social self.

        1) Give everyone an identical sheet of paper. Ask them to write the phrase, "I suspect that most people in this group see me as _____," at the top of the page, and the phrase, "And/But I really am _____," across the middle of the sheet.

        2) Next, they are to complete these sentences as fully as possible using adjectives, descriptive phrases, a short paragraph, etc. They *don't* write their names on this.

        3) Papers are folded and passed to the leader. Read top half of one aloud. Ask group to guess who wrote it. Individual identifies himself or herself. Then read bottom half. Encourage discussion of discrepancies before moving on.

    b. This exercise will allow unexpressed feedback to be aired.

        1) Distribute blank sheets of paper. Ask each person to tear it into quarters and to write a note to four people in the group communicating messages that have been withheld during the semester. Examples are:

            (a) Situations when you felt especially warm, friendly, close to that person

            (b) Situations when you felt irritated, in disagreement, disappointed with the other person

            (c) Situations when you learned something from the other person

            (d) Something you wanted to say to the other person, but couldn't get into the flow of conversation or felt hesitant to express

       (e) Something you would like to have happen between you and the other person in future sessions or outside of class

       (f) A question you'd like to ask

       (g) Something you'd like to share about yourself

       (h) Anything else that would deepen your mutual understanding or make your relationship more honest and open.

    2) Participants fold and address their messages. Collect and distribute them. After they have been read, ask each person to comment to each sender on what was received, even if it is just "Thanks for the note." Discussions are welcome.

  c. Ask each person to jot down answer(s) to each of the following questions, then develop single group answers, one by one:

    1) What single change would most improve this course next semester (with respect to lecture, group work, outside assignments)? Why?

    2) What single change should be suggested to the chancellor of the university? Why?

    3) Should our last class session be held or cancelled?

    4) What should we do during our group's time at the last class session? Why?

    5) If we had to give our group a name or title, what would it be? Why?

Self-Aid

Lecture Review Question

We discussed a number of approaches to self-aiding. If you were to become "your own best friend" what three to five actions would you take to help yourself better meet your needs at this time in your life?

Group Review Question

Identify something you did in the group to help yourself benefit more from it. Also, identify something you thought about doing but did not do because of others' expectations.

Dyad Activity

You have had ten dyad experiences thus far. By this time you probably have some sense of the kinds of experience most useful for you. Consequently, since our theme is self-aid, you have the option of determining what human relations experience you will have this week. Each of you should be in charge of one-half hour of your time together; the other will try to cooperate in fulfilling your needs.

The first person should begin by stating your goal for the time period (e.g., becoming better acquainted, having a relaxing conversation, exploring an issue in depth, straightening out your relationship, etc.). Then, he or she should describe the means or procedure for achieving the goal as well as making any additional suggestions along the way to help keep you both on target. That person is responsible for making sure that his or her half of the dyad is selfishly worthwhile.

Reverse roles for the second half. The second person then determines what should happen for the dyad to be worthwhile for him or her, and the first person cooperates.

Dyad Review Question

Summarize what each of you did, how it felt to take responsibility for stating your needs and to ask for help in meeting them, and how what occurred relates to your everday life.

What can a person do through just talking to help someone who is puzzled, depressed, hurt, scared, upset, or in any other disturbed state?

To answer this question, think about a time when someone helped *you* through such an experience and recall what he or she actually did.

Group Exercises

a. An important aspect of self-care is asking for help from others. Help can come in several ways:

1) Sharing of similar experiences
2) Offering advice
3) Listening with caring and empathy
4) Offering feedback based on what has happened in the group or dyads
5) Pointing out contradictions, discrepancies, errors in thinking
6) Identifying options or choices in a situation
7) Evaluating choices — how each might work out
8) Tuning into one's deeper feelings about things

    (a) Ask students to recall their goals for this course *or* to list the people in their lives and identify how they would like to grow in any of their in-group or outside relationships.

    (b) Ask them to share the problem situation with the group.

    (c) Select from the list given the kind(s) of help they want and request it of the group (or a particular individual).

    (d) Question the helpers for more information and say, "Thank you," to end the discussion with each person.

b. Ask people to share and gain group participation in their own "feel-good" activity (e.g., yoga, singing, massage, folk dance, drawing, meditation).

c. Ask everyone in the group to make a list of which situations create the following feelings and ways in which they help themselves move into such feelings. Then share what they have written.

1) cared for
2) excited
3) confident
4) relaxed
5) proud
6) challenged
7) having fun
8) peaceful, spiritual

Aiding Others

Lecture Review Question

This last review assignment covers the entire course. Jot down brief answers to these questions:

a. What idea introduced in the lectures do you most want to retain and employ in your life?
b. What group experience meant the most to you?
c. What concept from your reading this semester was most significant to you?
d. What experience in a dyad was most meaningful to you?
e. What is one way that the lectures could be improved?

f. What is one way that a group exercise could be improved?

g. What is one way your group leaders were helpful to you?

h. What is one thing your group leaders could have done better?

i. What is one way the assignments and grading system could have been better?

Group Review Question

We discussed in class several features of helpful communication which you attempted to apply in your group session. Evaluate what was advocated in your group session. Evaluate what was advocated in the lecture by comparing it to helpful situations you have experienced this semester, in or out of class. Did those principles generally apply in reality?

Dyad Activity

This activity can, once again, be done with anyone in your group, this class, or elsewhere who would be willing to share this experience with you.

Each of you should be ready for the session by completing the following sentences:

a. I feel least comfortable with someone who _____.

b. A situation that might benefit me, but that I tend to avoid is _____.

c. A topic that I find hard to talk about is _____.

d. A recent experience in which I felt even mildly upset, hurt, scared, angry, or disappointed was _____.

Your answers should suggest issues on which you might need some help. Pick one of these to work on during this session.

For the first half of your time together one of you is to be the helper and the other is to work on his or her problem area, i.e., be a helpee. Then you will switch roles. Decide the order in which you will assume these roles.

The helpee need only be available to explore issue(s) as fully as he or she can or wishes.

The helper has the responsibility of giving the helpee full, caring attention, making the other feel comfortable about being open and honest, aiding the helpee to think through the internal and external pressures influencing him or her, expressing feelings, identifying goal(s) and evaluating alternative approaches for improving things. The helper should be as genuine as possible while trying to carry out some of the suggestions offered in the lecture.

Each half might last about 20 minutes, or until the helpee's situation has been fully discussed to your mutual satisfaction. After each half, take a few minutes to discuss what happened between you.

Group Exercises

a. Ask participants to draw a personal group history line as indicated, dividing it into meaningful segments, citing turning points:

First class session _____ Now

b. Discuss these questions:

1) Which course theme meant the most to you?

2) Which books did you read? Would you recommend them to others?

3) About whom in the group has your opinion changed most?

82

4) What is something you learned about yourself?

5) In what way do you now see yourself as more similar to others in your group?

c. Since this is the last session, consider what gift you would like to give each person in your group. Focus on one person at a time and have everyone else think of something he or she would like to give (or exchange with) that person.

d. Divide the group into halves or thirds and ask each subgroup to create a closing experience for the whole.

e. Divide the group into halves or thirds and allow the subgroups 10 minutes to use themselves, others, and/or any props in the area to create a nonverbal expression of an idea or feeling that was important to the group.

f. Discuss what each person will do in the near future and how concepts from this course might be used.

g. Using masking tape and paper, tape one blank sheet on each person's back. Invite participants to list a new growth or strength on one another's papers. Sheets become nice souvenirs.

CHAPTER 5

Soft Listening

I

It has long been acknowledged that listening is a crucial element in the process of communication and that it merits a central place among the curricula of communication education. Innumerable attempts have been made to articulate what an individual needs to know and do in order to improve his or her ability to listen. Virtually all approaches (including this one) assume that listening occurs:

> as a result of a constellation of psychological and physical behaviors,
> affecting both speaker and listener,
> which vary depending upon the purpose of their interaction.
> Some behaviors impede achievement of these purposes, others enhance it, and the latter can be learned.

Consequently, in order to develop an approach to listening instruction, one needs to identify the interactive intent, the behaviors which facilitate achieving that goal, and how they can be taught. That, in sum, is the purpose of this chapter.

II

The history of listening training parallels that of speech instruction. Traditionally, both were concerned with public communication—the giving and receiving of speeches. Hence, the aims of listening were seen to complement the aims of speaking: to comprehend the content of informative talks, to critically appraise the content of persuasive talks, and to enjoy or appreciate talks intended to entertain.

More recently with the introduction of interpersonal communication to course catalogs, many new types of listening have been identified. They range in number from six[1] to forty.[2] There is no standard typology.

These category systems are inadequate, primarily because they are based upon only their creator's speculation and because they have little or no pragmatic utility, i.e., their definitions are not operational and they are too numerous to be usefully employed. People cannot realistically be expected, in the midst of spontaneous discourse, to switch consciously from one type of listening to another as often as necessary, choosing each time from a plethora of alternatives. A more parsimonious approach is necessary — one based, as well, on a somewhat objective system of viewing human behavior. To develop such a system we must begin at a very basic level.

A fundamental statement is that at any given moment a human being either *is* or *is not* listening. When not listening, one is either alone, sleeping, talking, or thinking about a past or imagined situation. These instances need not concern us.

When a person is in another's presence and is giving some attention to the other, listening is occurring. This includes a broad range of situations. To what extent must these be subdivided to achieve our criteria of parsimony and utility? To answer this, let us return to the dichotomy between hard and soft postures proposed in chapter 1. When an individual is listening to someone else, one of these two states may be said to predominate. Let me elaborate further on the characteristics of each orientation in order to clarify its nature. These characteristics may be divided into three dimensions: physiological, perceptual, and psychological.

A. Physiological Indicators

It may at first seem inappropriate to consider the state of one's body when discussing listening — especially if one considers listening to be primarily a mental "decoding" process, as it is usually depicted in communication literature. A fundamental assumption of the approach advocated here, however, is that one's entire organism is involved in the listening process. In fact, the physiological set of a receiver has a profound influence on what he or she is attuned to. In other words, the human being as listener may be thought of as a "transducer"—one who leads something across something else (e.g., as a microphone leads sound waves across air into electrical currents).[3]

The state of one's organism differs in many subtle but significant ways and therefore transduces incoming messages differently when one is in a soft versus a hard state of awareness.

When a soft approach to the environment is being taken, an individual's body is manifesting a constellation of physiological symptoms which may be viewed as components of a larger syndrome known as the "orienting response" (OR). These components include changes in the following body areas: in sense organs; in skeletal muscles directing sense organs; in skeletal musculature; in the central nervous system; and vegetative changes.[4]

When these and other factors are present, an individual's organism is optimally open to listening to messages sent him or her and to perceiving them as they are — as new information about a unique situation, as input to register and absorb, rather than as stimuli to which one must hastily respond.

Two kinds of orienting responses exist — phasic and tonic. Phasic ORs are short-lived, lasting only a few seconds. Tonic ORs can last as long as fifty minutes or more. Both heighten receptivity. However, the tonic OR may be viewed as setting the cerebral capacity to attend to sensory information demands. Generally speaking, the greater the tonic ORs triggered in an individual the more frequently phasic ORs will be triggered in response to the same stimulus.[5] Later, we will explore how specific listening exercises might help to arouse the tonic orienting response.

In addition to habituation,[6] in which listening behavior is numbed, the other physiological reaction to a stimulus is the "defense response" (DR). This is the physiological syndrome present when one is in a hard state. It is comparable to the "fight–flight" reaction mentioned earlier. Its symptoms are simply the reverse of those for an OR.

Traditional listening games that indicate how easily a message can become garbled when one is involved in a classroom exercise and intent upon passing it on to others serve to illustrate how the DR affects behavior. Procedures involving organizing one's thoughts, following main points, asking questions of the speaker, etc., have all been ways commonly suggested for coping with the screening effects of the DR.

In summary, when one is experiencing an OR, she/he is in a soft state; when a DR occurs, she/he is in a hard state. Since these states have physiological roots, they can be affected by physical activities, as we shall see later.

B. Perceptual Indicators

The presence of an OR or DR affects one's perception, hence one's listening, in several ways. Overall, the impact is on nonjudgmental openness. However, this global distinction between hard and soft, I believe, has a number of more specific manifestations. These include the following:

1. In a soft mode one's degree of perceptual "vigilance" is higher than when in a hard mode. Vigilance is an aspect of attention that is measured by the capacity to detect rare, near-threshold signals.[7] A soft person is, therefore, more "sensitive" to subtle

cues, to slight shifts in position, gesture, facial expression, tone of voice, etc. The opposite of vigilance has been termed "tenacity" of perception — focusing continuously, without availability to distraction, on a specific object. This quality applies more to a hard state.

2. In a soft mode one's perception is usually more "extensive," as opposed to being more "intensive" in the hard mode. This quality refers to the number of stimuli attended to at a given time. The soft perceiver is more "inclusive," the hard perceiver more "selective." As a result, someone in a soft posture is often attuned to a wider and deeper range of perceptions, to more levels of a sender's message — such as feelings, ambiguous meanings, essential causes of behavior — and to the points of view of several people in a group. His or her scope is broad, while a hard listener's range may be said to be "tunneled." This quality might be termed "holistic" listening, as distinguished from "segmented" listening, the latter being the strength of the hard position.

3. The presence of tonic ORs in a soft mode serves, as well, to extend the "time span" of a listener's attentiveness. Additional time given to the receptive process allows the soft listener to be perceived as a more "patient" receiver. Such a listener is more willing to hear out the full message of a speaker than is a listener in a hard position.

4. Likewise, in a soft position one is more prone to "delay making associative links." In other words, one is less likely to jump to conclusions than is someone in a hard mode. He or she is capable of collecting a larger storehouse of impressions before trying to synthesize them into a coherent message that fits one's frame of reference. He or she sees them all more freshly, not so quickly putting them into preformed categories in automatized, stereotypical patterns. This quality is appropriate to the listening posture of a helper, one who must grasp all the elements of a speaker's view of a situation before diagnosing or responding.

In sum, soft listening may be said to differ from hard in that it is the state in which one is more likely to be vigilant, extensive, patient, and to delay associations when attending to the message of another.

C. Psychological Indicators

One's physiological and perceptual states constantly affect one's thoughts and emotions, and vice versa. Consequently, there are corresponding distinctions between hard and soft positions in terms of one's mental state that relate to the levels described earlier. At the psychological level, the differences can also be broken down into several categories.

1. Human motivations are most globally subdivided into two major areas — the desire for influence (or power) and the desire for

intimacy (or love). Each of these concerns predominates in the hard and soft modes respectively. When listening in a hard mode, one is tuned primarily into issues affecting one's desires related to control. When listening in a soft mode, one is aware primarily of messages related to closeness.

2. There is some difference between the two modes in terms of the degree of pressure with which needs are felt. A hard orientation is one concerned with effect, with impact. Thus, it is precipitated by a dissatisfied, desiring, aspiring stance, or the presence of "high need pressure" which severely affects listening. "High need pressure is the enemy of exploratory play and is a condition under which we are unable to achieve an objective grasp of the environment. Low need pressure is requisite if we are to perceive objects as they are, in their constant character, apart from hopes and fears we may at other times attach to them."[8]

3. Since a hard approach is concerned with controlling, doing, achieving, it is more oriented, as well, to "efficiency" than is a soft approach. Whereas a hard posture emphasizes structure and precision, fitting input into preestablished categories, a soft posture is more fluid, spontaneous, flexible, allowing the development of new perspectives, frames of reference, etc. Thus a soft approach is more useful for developing empathy, for hearing another individual's point of view which might be quite different from one's own. It is useful, too, for attending to messages that are less logical, based more on emotional issues.

4. A corollary to this last point is that an emphasis on impact, efficiency, reordering events — as exists in a hard stance — also leads to a discriminating, selective viewpoint. This supports a critical, prescriptive judgmental response. On the other hand, a soft stance lends itself to a more inclusive, tolerant, accepting perspective. This posture yields a more soothing, reassuring, warm response.

Perhaps one way we can sum up this category, and this whole section as well, is to pose two different sets of images for thought, one representing the hard and the other the soft listener. I picture for the former, in the interpersonal domain of communication, an employer listening to an applicant being interviewed for a job; a voter questioning a candidate for public office; a customer receiving a salesman's pitch; a worker listening to instructions from her/his boss; a father listening to his child ask a question posed in a homework assignment; a waiter taking an order in a restaurant, etc.

For the latter, the soft approach, I envision a counselor listening to a client describing her/his concerns; a congregation member querying a clergyman for advice about a problem; an audience member listening to a play, concert, or any event to be absorbed and appreciated; a husband or wife listening to his or her mate describe the events of the day; a listener to a friend's description of a recent trip or gratifying experience, etc.

For the epitome of the hard listener I picture Rodin's sculpture entitled *The Thinker,* someone tense with thought, struggling to move past where one is, to a point where a solution or insight emerges. As the epitome of the soft listener, I envision a statue of Buddha, someone serenely gazing at what is, open-faced, smiling slightly, wanting only to understand compassionately the scene before him, making no effort to change it.

III

Having described the two states of being from which listening might emerge, the next step is to identify further when each is best employed. What are the circumstances in which a hard posture is to be sought, and when is a soft posture most appropriate?

These circumstances are determined largely by the intentions of the listener, the speaker, and the situation in which they find themselves. It is evident that when each person is primarily goal-oriented, i.e., seeking to achieve a specific end, a hard approach is more suitable; and that when each is seeking simply to enjoy the here-and-now experience of their interaction, a soft approach is the more appropriate one.

Communicators must beware of assuming too hastily the intent of the other. A mismatch often causes communication breakdown. This has been evident to me from observing innumerable discussions in interpersonal communication classes that are initiated by someone describing a problem situation he or she is facing. Usually, others, made somewhat uncomfortable by the speaker's distress and assuming that he or she wishes to alleviate the problematic conditions, listen from a hard posture. They quickly jump to conclusions about the predicament and begin to shower the speaker with advice about how things can be made better. They are chopping away (to return to my martial arts metaphor) at the problem. Quite often, the person was not seeking a hard response. He or she wanted primarily to be heard and understood. So he or she slips into a "defensive response" and then cannot see any new information in what is being offered. What a facilitator must do in this situation is to reorient at least one, or both, of the communicators to a softer, more open position.

The same mismatching occurs when a professor sets students into a soft position by delivering an informative lecutre whose contents they are to retain. They are expected to absorb, to take in the message. When the instructor stops and asks for questions or comments, students often are very slow to respond. They may appear apathetic or dull. A better explanation for the lethargy of their response is that they are being asked to shift immediately from a soft to a hard mode of thought — from a nondiscriminating, receptive mode to a critical or selective one. This involves a global physiological, perceptual, and psychological shift, as has been described.

Not only does the intention of a listener and/or speaker affect the mode adopted, but the environmental constraints influence the choice, as well. There are times when divergent thinking (a soft mode of thought) is encouraged and times when convergent processes (a hard mode) are optimal.

When a question of fact is being considered wherein a single right answer exists, when a decision must be reached quickly, or when a method or procedure is emerging from a discussion as most obvious, a hard mode is preferable. When a question of policy or value is being discussed, ample time is available, and no clearcut answer is apparent, a soft mode is appropriate.

When a personal issue has been raised that involves feelings as well as facts, especially one that arises out of a complex situation in which many people's interests are involved, a soft listener is most useful. Often in such a situation all of the available options are already apparent to the speaker, and all that remains is making a choice that he or she and the others involved can best live with. Here, there is nothing to be done by the listener. He or she need simply be someone in whose caring presence the speaker can solve his or her own problem or make his or her own decision, i.e., the listener needs to be soft.

At other times, there is little flexibility, either because of the few choices available or a power imbalance that puts one person in a super-ordinate position to another. When an individual in this case is confused, he or she needs a decisive hard listener. However, once a step has been taken or an irreversible condition exists, and the only task left is to accept it, then a compassionate, soft listener is needed.

Thus, it behooves participants in an interaction to inform one another or to identify for themselves whether they are seeking either understanding and/or nonjudgmental consideration of many points of view (calling for soft listening) or a discriminating, goal-oriented, critical response (calling for hard listening).

IV

We have divided modes of listening into two categories and discussed when each might better be used. Of course, people do not have inner light switches with which to shift from one to the other, nor does either exist in a simple on/off form. Consequently, there needs to be some consideration of how the two modes interact.

There are several possible answers to this question. One is that they operate in alternation, depending on situational demands, as described. This alternation can vary from moment to moment in the course of a conversation, or each might predominate in major segments of time (e.g., when on vacation or at home, when at work).

There are points at which both seem to be active and somehow well integrated with each other. This does not occur very often, but it may serve to distinguish a state called "creative" listening, when hard and soft qualities seem equally available to the listener.

At times, I feel available only to listening passively (softly) to a message or presentation that demands no response from me. At other times, I am too restless to do so; I must react, do something about a situation I can tolerate no longer. At a third point, I feel almost equally available to either option, both fully receptive to what is being said and simultaneously processing, almost unconsciously, a subsequent action to be employed when a move on my part seems intuitively appropriate. The last state, with both options available, seems to be the most effective.

Usually, however, one mode or the other is preeminent. Most often, I see the hard mode as dominant. During an interactive sequence, most people, especially students, seem to find it easier to listen in a truly receptive fashion for only a short period of time before they begin rehearsing or articulating a response proposing that some action be taken. Perhaps this is because they have been conditioned to believe that doing, giving out, solving, answering, or some other overt activity is the optimal way of responding to an uncertain situation. Ours is an "output"-oriented society. Few people exhibit the patience, awareness, and comprehensiveness of thought to absorb a complex verbalization without turning off their orienting response. They come to a quick conclusion about what is being said by placing it into a familiar category, and then wait impatiently to respond, especially when a problematic situation is being described.

At such moments, however, each mode has its own kind of usefulness. They may be said to be "complementary" in the sense that Niels Bohr used the term to describe how the phenomenon of light could be viewed. From two different conditions of observation one can develop conclusions that seem incompatible (e.g., that light behaves as if it were composed of discrete particles in some experiments and in others as if it were a continuous wave) but which are equally accurate. Their incompatibility is only a function of the different conditions of observation. Thus, when one changes one's organismic program from intake (soft) to manipulation (hard), one's perceptions and view of a situation will differ but both views have validity and potential utility.

Consequently, it is useful to learn how to handle this shift from mode to mode consciously and comfortably so as not to approach a listening situation inappropriately, and even to have both modes at one's disposal from one moment to the next as conditions change.

Perhaps guidance as to the choice and use of each mode can come ultimately only from the source Saint Theresa of Avila consulted in her famous prayer: "Lord, grant me the serenity to accept the things I cannot change, the courage to change the things I can, and the wisdom to know the difference."

V

I have claimed, thus far, that there are two salient operationally defined types of listening: hard and soft. The former seems to dominate, both in what is discussed in the traditional literature on listening and in people's habitual approach to the role of listener. Heretofore it has been assumed that people most often are goal-oriented (hard) and that listening instruction should be designed to assist them in this pursuit. Hence, extant text material on listening emphasizes methods of achieving a variety of communication goals through listening. Since this approach is so well covered elsewhere, it would be redundant to repeat it here.

Soft listening is less widely discussed. In practice, at least in our culture, it seems to be subordinate to, less often reinforced than, a hard approach. The current challenge, I believe, to innovation in listening instruction is to define and transmit skills for shifting from a hard to a soft approach to listening.

The process by which this transformation might be accomplished is not as yet fully explored in any one source. This is not surprising since the constructs developed in this chapter have not been utilized elsewhere in discussions of listening. The techniques suggested will seem familiar, however, since they are all borrowed from systems of personal growth that have as their primary focus other dimensions of human behavior. In other words, to speculate about what a process for shifting listening states might entail, I have looked to procedures advocated in several closely related spheres, those with which this view of listening has much common ground.

My hypotheses about this process are not based upon empirical studies that I or others have done on listening behavior. These do not exist. Instead, they have been synthesized from more personal sources, including my own long-standing interest in and attentiveness to listening as a factor in communication, years of reading and efforts to develop my own ability in this domain, and several attempts to teach the underlying skills to others.

In other words, for a long time I found myself drawn to learning more about the methods to be described and intuitively sensed their applicability to my work, although they have not usually been seen as means for communication instruction. I suspected a connection as I discovered that with practice and development of my ability to implement them, my competence as a communicator grew — particularly in the domain of receptive listening. In fact, the development of the constructs discussed in this chapter was motivated, in large part, by a desire to conceptualize superordinate principles that would lend coherence to these two apparently related phenomena. The validity of the constructs and the methods of operationalizing them thus far has been demonstrated by the approbation of colleagues and the statements of students who report experiencing growth in the desired direction.

To be specific, I have found that soft listening is the result of assuming a posture toward others composed of a number of essential characteristics, each of which can be a target of instruction. These characteristics and the instructional methodologies can be conceptualized as falling within the same categories used earlier: physiological, perceptual, and psychological. In fact, my experience indicates that the pedagogical sequence for approaching this skill follows the same order.

The first dimension to be considered is the physiological set for soft listening. A process for developing one's organism to be an optimal transducer for soft listening can be extrapolated from several sources. Recently much attention has been given to the effect of somatic states on the processing of information. This concern emerges from a new awareness of mind-body integration. It is manifested in literature dealing with topics such as reducing stress caused by the pressures of life in modern society, utilizing the unique capacities of one's right and left brain hemispheres, and achieving optimal good health by drawing upon physical disciplines developed in other parts of the world, particularly the Orient.

Each of the aforementioned movements seems to have aims that coincide with those of this chapter, developing an appreciative, receptive stance toward one's environment. Consequently, it seems likely (both logically and, from my own experience, phenomenologically) that work along these same lines would enhance development of tonic orienting responses, i.e., the physiological syndrome of soft listening. What then are ways of teaching an individual to induce voluntarily in oneself the somatic state present in soft listening?

These ways seem to fall into three categories: methods for enhancing relaxation; a free flow of energy; and a centered, grounded posture. To make these categories a useful part of a communication instructor's repertoire, each is briefly defined and methods for inducing each state are introduced. (Please note that the explanation of each method provided here is not intended to be sufficiently comprehensive to prepare an instructor to develop competence in implementing it. Since they weren't invented for this purpose — each is drawn from an already existing system of personal growth — other sources are better suited for obtaining detailed explanations. Hence, several optional approaches are proposed under each heading, and more appropriate sources are briefly quoted or cited for each from which fuller accounts can be obtained.)

A. Relaxation describes a state in which muscles and nerves are temporarily at rest. Its physiological effects, such as decreased oxygen consumption, respiratory rate, heart rate, blood pressure, muscle tension, etc., are in opposition to or counteract those of the defensive or fight-flight response. Three common methods of inducing a relaxed state are cited:

1. Progressive Relaxation

   a) Begin by lying down on your back on the floor, arms at your sides. Close your eyes.

   b) Become aware of your breathing. Try not to change it, but rather just allow yourself to listen to it. If you like, locate the place on your torso where you feel the rising and falling of each breath.

   c) Begin by tightening your hands into fists, then let them go. Repeat 2-3 times, allowing yourself plenty of time to experience the release.

   d) Tighten your arms and let them go. Do not make your hands into fists, but allow them to remain flat on the floor. You may want to bring your hands up to your shoulders and let them go for variation, especially if you are sitting rather than lying down. Repeat 2–3 times, again allowing yourself enough time to experience the release.

e) Curl your toes and let them go. Repeat 2–3 times.

f) Tighten your legs and let them go. Again, if you are sitting, you might want to bring your knees toward your chest and then let them go. Repeat 2–3 times.

g) Tighten the stomach and pelvic area and let it go. Repeat 2–3 times.

h) Tighten the face as a whole or part by part, and let it go. Repeat 2–3 times.

i) Tighten your whole body and let it go. "Give your whole body a hug."

j) Check your breath (b) and see if it is any lower or deeper than when you started the exercise.[9]

2. Breathing

Find a quiet place to lie down. Center your breathing. Try breathing in and out through various parts of your body. Examples: up your toes and into your legs; down your legs and out your toes; up your fingertips and into your arms; down your arms and out your fingertips. Breathe in and out of your upper back. Give yourself plenty of time to experience the process. Become aware of any sensations such as color or temperature so that you may experience the area that is "breathing." Note: Center your breathing after working on each area.[10]

3. The Relaxation Response

a) Sit quietly in a comfortable position.

b) Close your eyes.

c) Deeply relax all your muscles, beginning at your feet and progressing up to your face. Keep them relaxed.

d) Breathe through your nose. Become aware of your breathing. As you breathe out, say the word, "ONE," silently to yourself. For example, breath IN . . . OUT, "ONE"; IN . . . OUT, "ONE"; etc. Breathe easily and naturally.

e) Continue for 10 to 20 minutes. You may open your eyes to check the time, but do not use an alarm. When you finish, sit quietly for several minutes, at first with your eyes closed and later with your eyes opened. Do not stand up for a few minutes.

f) Do not worry about whether you are successful in achieving a deep level of relaxation. Maintain a passive attitude and permit relaxation to occur at its own pace. When distracting thoughts occur, try to ignore them by not dwelling upon them and return to repeating "ONE." With practice, the response should come with little effort. Practice the technique once or twice daily, but not within two hours after any meal, since the digestive processes seem to interfere with the elicitation of the Relaxation Response.[11]

B. A free flow of energy is difficult to define. It might be thought of as a loose, limber, alert state. It often accompanies relaxation, but not necessarily. One can be relaxed and soporific. I am referring instead to a poised, attentive, flexible quality of ease, wherein one is consciously aware of one's own physical being and is awake and responsive to the other. It is likely to produce many of the physiological conditions of the orienting response. This sense of aliveness and well-being can be the product of several exercise systems such as the three I have listed.

1. Hatha yoga — especially the Salute to the Sun postures — a series of twelve asanas which are fully described in any book that deals with yoga.[12]

2. Arica gym — another series of energizing exercises drawn from many sources.[13]

3. Calisthenics — the standard gymnastic exercises that are performed in physical education classes to loosen and warm up participants (not those intended to build muscular strength).

C. A centered, grounded posture also is more readily experienced than defined verbally. This concept is discussed in descriptions of the soft martial arts, such as *aikido*. They suggest that the center of one's strength is located in the *hara,* a point in the middle of the abdomen about two inches below the navel.

> Your *hara* is situated in the middle of your body and is the vital mid-point which balances the upper and lower portions of your body. It is like the center point of a teeter-totter, except, of course, that your body is vertical. Situated at the mid-point, your *hara* is relatively stable and constant in terms of movement and, therefore, it is the center of balance for your entire body.[14]

> One method of locating it is to let all the air out of your lungs by exhaling or yelling; the point of pain . . . [is] the *hara*. The simplest way of locating it, however, is to bend over from the waist. The *hara* is located at the crease.[15]

When one is aware of this point and views it as the source of one's actions, one is more balanced, more firmly rooted in one's position, less likely to react impulsively to, or (figuratively) to grasp or to push away a person with whom one is dealing. In times of nervous tension, people unconsciously take deep breaths to relieve tension. This causes them to focus on their hara. When most Occidental people are asked to point to the place in their bodies where their "locus of control" exists, they usually indicate the head or the heart. Japanese people, aware of the hara tradition, will point to their stomachs. The anchoring, pacifying, softening effect of a low center of gravity (which makes one less of a "pushover") is the reason meditation is usually done in a "lotus" position (seated in cross-legged fashion). This specific posture is not essential for soft listening; but assuming a comfortable, familiar, balanced, seated position, with an erect spine (to maintain alertness) can be an important aid to maintaining the relaxed, yet alert receptivity this process demands. Exercises for becoming more centered or grounded include those provided in the following systems:

1. Aikido

The teacher begins by asking participants to sit and rise in their accustomed manner. For most of them, this entails leading with their eyes, chin, neck or shoulders. In our head-oriented society, the command "rise" or "sit" generally seems to come from somewhere within the cranium, placing undue energy awareness in the top part of the body. The teacher suggests that the participants concentrate awareness in the center of the belly, the *hara,* to think of the *hara* as moving up and down while the rest of the body, entirely relaxed, simply goes along for the ride. Most of them find that this requires much less effort than before.

The teacher takes them a step further. He suggests that they put their center of command in the *hara,* and just sit and wait until the *hara* itself says, "Rise." Those who can reach this level of energy awareness find themselves rising and sitting with no conscious effort. The upward motion is like levitation.

The teacher adds pressure. He asks half the partners to stand behind the other participants, to put hands on their shoulders and hold them down with an unvarying amount of pressure, say about ten to fifteen pounds. First, the participants concentrate their awareness on the hands on their shoulders instead of the *hara.* In this case, they find rising rather difficult. They then return their awareness to *hara* and make it the center of command. They do not deny the reality of the weight on their shoulders, but they consider it of no great importance. The partners apply the same force as in the earlier part of the exercise. In this case, however, almost all the participants rise easily. The difference is obvious. Some of the participants, in fact, ask their partners to add more and more pressure, and find themselves rising with little effort under forces that previously would have stuck them fast to their seats.[16]

2. Zen Meditation

The most important thing in taking the zazen posture is to keep your spine straight. Your ears and your shoulders should be on one line. Relax your shoulders, and push up towards the ceiling with the back of your head. And you should pull your chin in. When your chin is tilted up, you have no strength in your posture; you are probably dreaming. Also to gain strength in your posture, press your diaphragm down towards your *hara* or lower abdomen. This will help you maintain your physical and mental balance. When you try to keep this posture, at first you may find some difficulty breathing naturally, but when you get accustomed to it you will be able to breathe naturally and deeply.[17]

3. Physical Centering

Stand with your feet pointed forward, shoulder width apart. Unlock your knees so that your legs are flexed. Close your eyes, and from your feet — not from your waist — begin to move as far in a clockwise direction as you can without falling over. Move slowly, with one full inhalation and exhalation each time you go around in a circle, exhaling as you go through the front half of your circle and inhaling as you go through the back half.

When you've fully turned in to the rhythm of your circular movement, gradually make your circle smaller, continuing to coordinate your breathing and movement, until your circle becomes very tiny. Be sure your head is erect and that your shoulders are loose.

Now stop at the center of your circle, where you are perfectly centered in relation to gravity. Check this by moving slightly forward, then back, then to the right and left, then back to the place of perfect balance, your knees still slightly flexed. Then take three deep, slow breaths. As you do, feel any tension that's left in your mind and body flow out with your outgoing breath, and let a sense of complete well-being flow in with your incoming breath.[18]

The *perceptual* set for soft listening seems most harmonious with two approaches to personal growth that I have encountered: Buddhist meditation and Gestalt therapy.

The former is a traditional practice based on a philosophy in which the object of personal development may be said to be seeing things as they are, from moment to moment, without judgment, observing and accepting change as it occurs, demanding nothing, and sensing one's own commonality with (rather than distinctiveness from) the process being perceived. The one quality of perception that is the basis and foundation of this viewpoint is expressed as "bare attention." This state of unobtrusive receptivity is eloquently described in many Buddhist texts. As a sample of how it might be articulated, allow me to quote a Western teacher of meditation with whom I have studied:

Bare attention means observing things as they are, without choosing, without comparing, without evaluating, without laying our projections and expectations on to what is happening; cultivating instead a choiceless and non-interfering awareness.

This quality of bare attention is well expressed by a famous Japanese haiku:

The old pond.
A frog jumps in.
Plop!

No dramatic description of the sunset and the peaceful evening sky over the pond and how beautiful it was. Just a crystal clear perception of what it was that happened. . . .

As bare attention is cultivated more and more we learn to experience our thoughts and feelings, situations and other people, without the tension of attachment or aversion. We begin to have a full and total experience of what it is that's happening, with a restful and balanced mind. . . .

There's a beautiful poem by a Zen nun:

Sixty-six times have these eyes beheld the changing scenes of autumn.
I have said enough about moonlight; ask me no more.
Only listen to the voice of pines and cedars when no wind stirs.

To hear the sounds of the trees when no wind stirs. The peacefulness of that mind expresses the balance of the Tao, the creative and receptive. It is creative in the sense of being alert, penetrating and actively attentive. It is receptive in its choicelessness, without discriminating or judging. It is a very open and soft mind. When alertness and clarity of perception are combined with receptivity and acceptance, the balance becomes complete, and the mind experiences a perfect harmony of poise and equilibrium.

There are two mental factors which are primarily responsible for the development of bare attention. The first is concentration, the ability of the mind to stay steady on an object. The other factor is mindfulness, which notices what is happening in the moment, not allowing the mind to become forgetful; it keeps the mind grounded and collected. When mindfulness and concentration are both developed, a balance of mind is achieved, and a profound listening occurs.[19]

Bare attention is another way of viewing the perceptual orientation of a soft listener. The fundamental method for developing this capacity is the practice of meditation. This is a widely taught process, approached in many ways.

There are literally hundreds of practices which can be listed under the heading of "meditation." All of these have in common the ability to bring about a special kind of free-floating attention. . . . It is characteristic of this state that when in it, the person is completely absorbed by his or her particular object of meditation.

. . . The devices used to bring about this state are as diverse as gazing quietly at a candle flame; attending to the mental repetition of a sound (*mantra*); following one's own breathing; concentrating on the imagined sound of rainfall; chanting out loud a ritual word or phrase; attending to body sensations; concentrating on an unanswerable riddle (*koan*); passively witnessing the flow of thoughts through one's mind; or whirling in a stereotyped dance. Whatever, the aim is the same: to alter the way the meditator experiences his or her own existence.[20]

It is beyond the scope of this chapter to provide explicit instruction in meditation since that is so readily available elsewhere. It is my intention, primarily, to recommend it as an extremely valuable method for the development of soft listening. In addition, I wish to offer two guidelines for discriminating from among the methods available in other sources those most relevant to the improvement of listening. First, the primary thrust of the instruction should be on the development of improved perception or awareness, not on the indoctrination of a set of religious beliefs. Second, the approach chosen should direct the attention of the meditator outward, toward heightened consciousness of one's environment, rather than inward toward shutting out external stimuli. With these two criteria in mind, I suggest that a beginner look to the practices of Zen meditation, Vipassana or insight meditation, or Krishnamurti's approach to meditation.

The second system that advocates a compatible perceptual stance is Gestalt therapy. This approach, to a large extent, equates mental health with attunement to one's here and now reality. Indeed, deviations from a receptively aware state are indications of a need to avoid or distort what is occurring. Hence, emphasis in the therapeutic process is given to helping individuals maintain persistent attention to their ongoing experience of themselves and their environment. Training in this process has been offered profitably to people seeking not therapy but personal growth in their ability to be fully awake to their moment-to-moment perceptions. The following is an example of how such training might be conducted:

> For a single session with a large group, I begin with a brief abstract statement of the awareness concept, then I form a small circle of six to eight volunteers in front of the larger group (in a smaller group, of course, everyone joins the circle). The starting situation is quite similar no matter how large the group, how many meetings are anticipated, or who the members are. Individuals in the group are asked to take a few minutes each, simply to begin a few sentences with "Now I am aware that _____." No further instructions are offered, and feedback from other group members and the leader is minimized during the first round of this experiment. The leader will occasionally assist an individual through a long hesitation by asking, "What are you experiencing now?" or just "And now?" Direct questions to the leader or another person — for example, "Is this right?" "What do you think?" etc. — are simply rephrased into the suggested format. "Now I am aware of wondering if I am doing this correctly." "Now I am aware of wanting to ask _____." The first two or three times that an individual seems to run down and show signs of wishing to stop, I try to help him report this experience of running down and wishing to stop. "My mind is blank, I can't go on," becomes "Now I am aware of feeling blank and unable to go on," but after two or three such assists, I terminate with one person and go on to the next.[21]

The final dimension of soft listening is the *psychological* set of the individual in this position. The conceptualization I have found most useful for articulating what such a set would entail is the description by Carl Rogers of the characteristics of an effective therapist. He identified three core elements: empathy, unconditional positive regard, and genuineness.[22]

The first, empathy, is concern for knowing how someone else feels, thinks, and perceives things from that person's frame of reference, to sense what the person is trying to say, to put oneself in the other's shoes. The second, unconditional positive regard, may be stated as caring, prizing, valuing, or respecting the other as a person of worth, without judgment or evaluation; accepting one for what one is, as one is, without demanding that one change or be different. The third, genuineness, means being real, open, sincere, not playing a role or being mysterious; relieving the other of any need to invest energy in figuring out how the listener is reacting; being transparent.

This theory has been translated into a set of behaviors that manifest this orientation operationally by Truax, Carkhuff, and Berenson. They divide the requisite skills into two categories: responsive and active. The former are those most useful for the development of soft listening. Exercises for increasing one's ability to perform each skill are now available in many books.[23]

To summarize, this section proposes that a needed addition to communication education in the realm of listening is instruction in developing the ability to shift from a hard to a soft listening posture. It was suggested that this instruction proceed in three stages: developing a physiological set (including relaxation, a free flow of energy, and a centered, grounded posture); developing a perceptual set (including bare attention and here-and-now awareness); and developing a psychological set (including empathy, unconditional positive regard, and genuineness).

The assumption behind this approach is that these three elements combine to create a posture on the listener's part that optimizes perceptiveness, receptivity, open-mindedness, and flexibility — traits commonly believed to be significant in the development of a fully competent communicator.

CHAPTER 6

Creative Synthesis: An Approach to a Neglected Dimension of Small Group Communication

I

Creativity is traditionally equated with the talent that guides a writer, a painter, a dancer, or any other artist in carrying out his/her work. This secret ingredient seems to entitle artists to special treatment. Their individualism is nurtured. People often smile at behavioral eccentricities of artists which would raise eyebrows if performed by other professionals. Artists, for example, are indulged, far more than ministers or teachers might be, when they choose to act or dress in an unorthodox way. This freedom from conformity hints at some common assumptions about the creative person.

One assumption is that the artist is autonomous. The praise, "He or she is a nice person," adds less to the evaluation of a painting than it would to judging the work of a minister or teacher. In fact, rudeness or intolerance in an artist is accepted, even vicariously enjoyed, perhaps because, in essence, his/her real work is done alone. Even if the artist is a theatrical director or choreographer, his or her concept and will can dominate; he or she may not have to adapt an interpersonal style to the needs of subordinates.

Also supporting the communication frailties of a creative artist is the assumption that he or she must feel free of all constraints which might inhibit the creative process. It is well understood that creativity demands unhampered manipulation of ideas and materials. This license often is extended to dealings with people.

During the most recent half of the twentieth century, however, much attention has been given to the role of creativity ouside the arts. The creation of new ideas and products is now viewed as vital for many aspects of personal and social growth. Change or freshness of experience is a need most people seem to experience with ever greater urgency. Individuals seek variety in their activities, apparel, home decor, in every aspect of their environment. Families need diversity in shared experiences to maintain their desire for cohesion. Organizations require fresh approaches for adapting to challenges presented by changing internal and external conditions. Societies must respond imaginatively to the ever-evolving demands of their citizenry. Ability in creative endeavors has clearly become a desirable asset for people in every domain of life.

In nonartistic areas, however, interpersonal coordination becomes more essential. The creativity demanded from committees, within families, among groups of friends and colleagues must be a collaborative effort. In these cases, an egocentric genius can hinder the process of group creativity as much as he or she can contribute to it.

Consequently, also in recent years, the role of group process has emerged as increasingly significant. The nuclear family, the modern organization, innovative teaching methods, all call for ever greater facility at group interaction. Indeed, a discipline of small group communication has been developed to meet this need.

Most of the work done in this discipline, however, is focused on two kinds of group tasks: problem-solving and personal growth. Literally thousands of studies and dozens of textbooks have been devoted to the procedures required for a group to arrive at an optimal or correct solution to a problem. Within the past decade an unprecedented series of articles, books, and workshops has been concerned with transactions that lead to actualizing human potential for intra- and interpersonal authenticity. At the University of Kansas, for example, a student can study in depth the dynamics of problem-solving groups and human relations groups. No course, however, is aimed at the dynamics of creativity in groups. The purpose of this chapter is to suggest a first step for incorporating this area into a course studying group communication.

II

Two areas must be addressed when examining creativity in groups: the goal of the creative act, or *what* is produced; and the process of "creative synthesis," or *how* the group works together to achieve its goal.

It may be said that there are two basic genres of creative products. One is *expressive* and the other is *problem-oriented*. They are distinguished chiefly by the criteria used for judging them. Expressive works are first evaluated by the degree of internal satisfaction experienced by those who produce them (unless the standards of a contest judge or a critic are being considered). Conversely problem-oriented creative achievements are successful when an externally based function is met.

Planning the decoration of a room or the creation of a dramatic improvisation are examples of expressive creativity. When the family feels that a room reflects how they wish their home to be seen, or when the cast feels that the improvised scene expresses their view of the situation to be depicted, it is successful. In both cases, the locus of evaluation is primarily internal.

Examples of problem-oriented creativity include designing a political poster and illustrating a book. In the first instance, the success of the venture is based on how many people vote for the candidate, and in the second how well the ideas in the book are complemented. These standards are external in origin.

Of course, the two domains are not mutually exclusive; they overlap in many ways. The source and means of evaluating creative output, however, are distinct, and this distinction suggests a different approach to the creative process. Training in group creativity should incorporate but differentiate both kinds of activities.

The process of creative synthesis may also be divided into two general categories, again depending on how it is to be judged. When people work together on a joint creative project, the effectiveness of their interaction may be evaluated by two criteria. The first is the *satisfaction* of the participants with what occurred during their collaboration. Few activities hook one's pride, or ego, and can leave one as exhilarated or deflated as a creative experience. When all members participate and feel that their contributions have been respected, the group can emerge from the experience feeling euphoric. When individuals clash without resolving their differences, feelings are hurt, often deeply. The continuing viability of a creativity group, therefore, is dependent upon the level of satisfaction participants report during and after the period of joint effort.

The second criterion for evaluating creative synthesis is the *quality* of the creative product. Ideas may be brought into harmonious unity, but if an extraordinary amount of time is taken to do so, or the group product is inferior to what any one individual could produce, then this criterion is not met. At times the group's struggle to reach consensus is so arduous and time-consuming that the issues are resolved only by reducing the product to the lowest common denominator, one that will neither offend, nor fully please anyone. When the participants' talents are combined effectively into a product that is beyond the capacity of any individual member, then true creative synthesis has been achieved.

In brief, a group process, in either expressive or problem-oriented creative tasks, that enhances member satisfaction and product quality is the aim of our study.

III

With this broad outline of one aspect of the group communication curriculum in mind, we can explore the development of creative ability and the best method of nurturing this learning in the classroom. Certain conditions in the practice of group creativity seem to mandate specific procedures in instruction.

When someone sits down to write an essay he/she usually can determine the time, place, and pace of the work. If one is uncertain about a specific procedure, one can stop, consult a reference work, and then proceed in whatever fashion is most comfortable. When a group meets to collaborate, however, its flexibility is severely limited. The circumstances and time of the meeting are vulnerable to the constraints of each participant's schedule. When an idea is thrown out, it usually must be responded to spontaneously, without the opportunity to rely on notes or other external sources of information. Thus, the knowledge or skills to be applied in this context must be learned deeply; they must be thoroughly internalized in order to be brought to bear at the instant they are needed. It is inappropriate, therefore, to expect students to learn what is required for effective group creativity by passively reading a book or hearing a lecture. The aims of this learning must be pursued actively, by genuine involvement in the process studied. Consequently, the first principle of instruction in group creativity is that it be *experiential*.

Yet, simply doing is not sufficient. When a group is actively engaging in creative synthesis its focus of attention is the project on which it is working. The dynamics of what transpires between members usually is ignored, even when productivity has broken down and interpersonal conflicts surface. If the group is unsuccessful, members usually blame their failure on the nature of their task, the personalities of the people, the condition of their tools, or anything else that is handy. Rarely can they pinpoint the interpersonal transactions that triggered or multiplied their difficulties. The second principle of instruction, therefore, is to provide a vehicle and an opportunity to *reexamine what transpired* in the group process that affected its success.

Every experience in group creativity involves a mixture of a great many variables. The size of the group, the personalities of its members, the nature of its task, the time available, the materials and countless other facets of the situation interact to make each instance virtually unique. Although a great many hypotheses have been posed about the creative process and much research has been conducted to test them, little that is definitive has been found. Many general guidelines exist which, if appropriately employed, can aid a participant to enhance the effectiveness of a group's creative effort. These should not be learned as rules. Instead, each is best examined for relevance to a specific group context in which a student may be involved. One can then determine their degree of usefulness and gain a feel for how such guidelines might be applied.

These suggestions point to a pedagogical approach involving a variety of creative tasks to be performed in groups, followed by reexamination of what occurred in the light of one or more hypotheses about the process. If the notion under consideration seems to apply fruitfully to the experience being examined, it can then be kept in mind during subsequent creative encounters for continuing consideration and refinement.

In summary, the instructional procedure advocated here for developing insight into the dynamics of creative synthesis is a highly experiential one in which a series of varied creative tasks is undertaken by small groups of students, each to be followed by a period of discussion. Each discussion session should, in turn, focus on a different dimension of the group interaction.

IV

In order to design a plan for a series of lessons in accordance with this experiential approach, we need to further specify the creative tasks and interaction hypotheses to be employed. Both areas may be divided in many ways. I have found the divisions sketched in this section to be useful.

As stated earlier, *creative tasks* may be divided into those with expressive and those with problem-oriented goals. One might further divide expressive tasks into *verbal* and *nonverbal* categories. Verbal tasks, involving language, include writing a poem or a song, writing a story, a fable, a slogan, or a caption, acting improvisations, and impromptu speeches. Nonverbal tasks include drawing a picture, creating a collage or a structure, pantomime, movement, etc. Many other activities, of course, could be added to these lists.

Problem-oriented creative tasks include finding new uses for everyday objects, adapting to unusual circumstances, prophesying the future, reorganizing old structures, considering the consequences of an unexpected occurrence, suggesting improvements for existing creations, etc.

These divisions might be clarified by viewing them on a small matrix. Most creative tasks may be viewed as predominantly either expressive or problem-oriented and as either verbal or nonverbal.

	VERBAL	NONVERBAL
EXPRESSIVE	1	2
PROBLEM-ORIENTED	3	4

Examples of activities which fit in each of the numbered boxes might be: 1) a short story, 2) a drawing, 3) creating advertising slogans for a product, 4) playing charades.

Besides including experience in these four categories, decisions regarding tasks to use for classroom learning need to be made on several other bases as well. First, tasks should approximate as closely as possible creative activities in which students might be engaged *outside* of school or in their future professions. Many available creative games just don't seem real to students. This is a hard criterion to meet, but a significant one to work toward.

In addition, the task should involve *group pooling* of resources, ideas, or skills. Having each person in a group make a separate drawing encourages individual creativity, but does not prepare them for a situation, for example, in which a committee must agree on a symbol or poster to represent its organization. On the other hand, asking the group to create a single drawing incorporates the challenges of creative synthesis more fully.

An effective learning task should also allow group members' *communication styles* to emerge. While task descriptions should include some structure, enough leeway must be allowed for leaders, decisions, conflicts, feelings, etc., to surface in the group. These are elements that influence group effectiveness, elements that must be examined, and that are the focus of learning to be gained from the group communication course.

Finally, it would be best if each task could be completed, for the most part, in no more than fifteen minutes. This *brief time limit* allows for a follow-up discussion that can retrace all the steps taken by the group in working on a task. Sometimes the initial approach to attacking the creative problem determines the quality of all subsequent work. If too much time goes by before the process is reexamined, recall may be dim. In addition, brief tasks allow time for many work-discussion cycles in the class periods allotted to this unit of study.

Another dimension to consider in planning group creativity tasks is *sequence*. Since this can be a new way of working together for many students, the first activities they are asked to do should be relatively *easy* and *clear*, with more challenges being added as the series progresses. Earlier activities should also be a bit more *structured* with smaller, more explicit steps than those that follow. Finally, the sequence of tasks should move from less to more *self-expression*. Students generally find greater satisfaction from increasing personal investment and exposure in a group, although they may hesitate at first. Therefore, just as they are reluctant to relate their creative work to themselves in the beginning, they will be equally reluctant to return to more objective, less self-expressive tasks after they have dropped their inhibitions regarding personal involvement.

The two criteria suggested for sucessful *creative synthesis* were group satisfaction and product quality. These may be influenced by many factors in the group's interaction. The literature on group dynamics is a rich source of variables which should be examined for their influence on these goals. Some group phenomena to explore in the light of students' experience with joint creative tasks might be: the degree of each member's participation in the interaction; the amount of influence each exerted on the nature of the final product and how that influence was exerted; the way conflicts were resolved or decisions made along the way; how the overall task was divided among members and the role each played in getting it done; the atmosphere or climate of the group; the subgrouping that might have occurred; feelings that were aroused, the degree to which they were expressed, and how these feelings were handled; the norms of the group, or what was criticized and praised; and responses to evaluative comments.

Any of these suggestions can be the stimulus for a discussion among a group of students who have just completed a creative task together. Here, too, however, some guidelines need to be considered. First, the topics should be *sequenced* from those that are safe or nonthreatening to those that may involve a bit of risk. As trust builds within a group, the threshold of what is comfortable to share lowers to include more, and the issues for discussion should take the group's gradually expanding limits into account. What this usually means in practice is that objective questions about creativity or group process in general should precede discussion of what has occurred in the here and now of the group experience.

Maintaining *consistent group membership* throughout the experiences in the unit permits the development of group rapport which is necessary for productive feedback. In some instances, however, resistant members will attempt to divert the group from serious consideration of discussion questions. *Assistance from the teacher* on how to attack and stay with the focal issues usually works to make these discussion sessions worthwhile. If the students you work with cannot identify how group dynamics variables apply to their interaction, a particularly perceptive individual can be designated as an *observer* and be asked to sit outside to watch the group in its creative work, looking for the behaviors to be discussed. The observer's feedback could then kick off the subsequent discussion.

Rather than defining all these briefly phrased categories and concepts at length, it might be more useful to clarify them by developing examples of their use in a unit on creative synthesis.

The approach I have used in the past is to write a sequence of group tasks, alternating creative projects with discussion and feedback sessions. Each task is placed in separate envelopes which are numbered sequentially. The class is divided into groups, usually with about five members in each group. Each group is given a set of envelopes and is instructed to open one at a time following the numbered order, and to carry out the instructions contained therein. The instructions for one sequence of tasks are provided in the next section.

V

Envelope #1

In each of these envelopes is a task for your group to perform. Some ask you to do a brief creative project. Others suggest a topic to discuss related to how your group worked together. The purpose of undertaking these tasks is to learn how *groups* can most effectively collaborate on creative tasks and to learn more about your *own* feelings and behavior in this context.

The envelopes alternate between the two kinds of tasks. This one has a creative activity, the second has a discussion topic, the third has another creative activity, the fourth a discussion topic, and so on. Creation and discussion call for two different kinds of attitudes and ways of thinking. Please try to do your best on both, and try to make the switch each time as well as you can.

The first activity calls for you to imagine that you have taken on the responsibility of caring for two children, about eight and twelve years of age, in an enclosed room for several hours. This is a demanding challenge, since all you have been given to use in keeping them occupied are a few simple pieces of equipment (which are listed). Your task is to create as many activities as you can for them using *only* these materials.

You will be addressing this problem in two ways. First, spend about ten minutes on your own listing as many possible activities as you can on a sheet of paper. (Ask someone in the group to serve as timekeeper, notifying everyone when the time is up.)

After each of you has developed your own individual lists, rejoin the other members of your group for another ten-minute work session. This time you are to pool your individual lists and try developing new ideas that no one had thought of, but that come to mind as the group tosses around and builds upon what individuals suggest. As a result, you will also have a group list which combines all proposed and newly developed activities. (You will need to ask another person to serve as group secretary to record ideas as they are suggested.)

Materials available:

3 paper clips
2 pencils
1 paper cup
1 wrapped stick of chewing gum
1 ten-foot length of rope
1 paper bag

Note: These (or other) items can be included right in the envelope to give students concrete objects to manipulate.

Envelope #2

The value of group effort in the process of creative thinking cannot be assumed. Many people believe that they can do this kind of work much more effectively alone. They believe that a group exerts pressure toward conformity that stifles creativity and individual initiative. It can create self-consciousness or competition that is inhibiting. They say, Too many cooks spoil the broth.

On the other hand, creative thinking often involves taking a fresh look at a familiar process, seeing it from a new perspective, breaking out of old patterns of thought. A group of people at times can stimulate one another to think more creatively than each could alone by presenting several approaches which can then be combined in new ways. Individuals can pick up other ideas and take them a step further. This view might be summed up as "the output of a group is better than the sum of its parts."

Keeping these two points of view in mind, decide upon a *group* answer to the following question:

If you had only one ten-minute period to do another "creativity problem" very much like the one you just did, do you think you would do better if you spent that time working:

( ) individually

(check one)

( ) as a group

Explain your answer in writing.

Envelope #3

Please read aloud directions 1-6 before beginning:

1. Distribute one sheet of paper to each person in your group.
2. Each person should write a number on the upper right corner of the paper, using a different number for each person.
3. Each person should begin drawing on the piece of paper whatever or however he or she would like. Continue with this for about a minute — ask one person to be timekeeper.

4. At that point everyone should stop and place his or her paper in the center of the circle.
5. Each person should take from the pile another person's paper and make any contribution to it that he or she would like.
6. After another minute repeat this process, continuing until there have been as many rounds as there are people in the group.
7. After you have completed the small drawings, get a large sheet of paper and spend three minutes with everyone drawing on it simultaneously, *as a group*.

(Note: Included in this envelope should be several sheets of 8½ x 11" blank typing paper for the first part and perhaps some colored pencils or crayons. Have several larger sheets of paper or oak tag handy for #7. These drawings can be hung around the room for students to compare their group's work with that of other groups.)

Envelope #4

There are at least two kinds of creative tasks. One kind is problem-oriented, where you try to meet an external goal (e.g., entertaining two small children), and the other is expressive, where you create what pleases you (e.g., drawing on a blank sheet of paper).

Put the list you made in activity #1 and the pictures you just drew in activity #3 in the center of your group. Recall what you thought, felt, and did during each activity, and list the *differences* each of you and your group experienced between the two.

Envelope #3 provided another kind of contrast between individual creativity (steps #1-6) and group creativity (#7). Discuss any differences you experienced between the two and summarize them in writing.

Envelope #5

Take the pictures out of this envelope and lay them out in the center of your group. Each was cut out of a recent magazine. Select one of the pictures, and as a group write a brief story about what has occurred and/or what will occur among the people in the picture. Don't hesitate to use your imaginations freely with this task. (Note: Any provocative scenes cut from a magazine can be used for this exercise.)

Envelope #6

Distribute a copy of this sheet to everyone in your group.

Each person should read over the questions provided for discussion. Then you should proceed through them, as a group, discussing each in turn. If you wish to deal with any very briefly or to go into any at length, feel free to do so. They are intended to aid you in exploring the influence of one aspect of group dynamics, that of *participation*, on your group's effectiveness. Use any procedure that you think best for achieving this goal.

1. Who are the people who have participated most in these exercises?

2. Who have been the low participators? Do these people feel "in" or "outside" the group?
3. The second creative activity was pictorial or *nonverbal* and this third one was written or *verbal*. How (and why) did the difference between the two media affect any individual's participation?
4. Have there been any shifts in participation (e.g., high participators became quiet, low participators became more active)? If so, why did these changes occur?
5. How have the quieter people in your group been treated? How has their silence been interpreted? As consent? Disagreement? Disinterest? Fear, etc.?
6. Are there any patterns in who talks to whom? If so, is there an explanation for them?
7. How has each person's level of participation affected the two criteria mentioned earlier: individual *enjoyment* of the group experience and the *quality* of the group's work?
8. Recall your group's answers to the questions just discussed and summarize in writing what you have found about the influence of participation on group creativity. (Each person should do this on individual copies of the sheet.)

Envelope #7

The purpose of this task is to apply your group's ability to inventing a creative activity. This confusing goal is made clearer in the steps outlined:

1. Begin by sharing a little bit of what each has done or felt about creative experiences in the past. Each member of the group should share with the others one *successful* creative experience he or she has had in his or her life, something that was enjoyed and/or well done. This might have been recent or early in childhood. Each person should also share either a time that he or she tried doing something creative that was *not* satisfying or something he or she would like to do, but has never tried.

   Remember, some people are able to be quite creative at home, in their work, or in a hobby although they may not recognize this. Creativity is not restricted to the arts — writing, painting, dance, etc. One may also be creative in interpersonal relationships and in many other ways, some of which may not be readily apparent.

   Go around your group being sure that each person has a chance to speak. It may be necessary for others to ask searching questions or to "tease out" areas and instances of individual creativity, as well as aspects of creativity about which one is dissatisfied.
2. Next, go around the group again, this time with everyone answering the question: What would you *now* like to do that would be creative and that you would enjoy doing with this group?

   After a minute of silence for thinking, each person should offer an opinion of what the group or individuals could do that would be fun and a chance to exercise their creativity.

110

3. Come to agreement as a group on what you would like to do in the next fifteen minutes, drawing from the suggestions just made. You might agree to take up one person's idea, to combine a few into one project, or to do several brief things. This is your decision to make.
4. The last step is simply to carry out your plan.

Envelope #8

Distribute a copy of this sheet to everyone in your group.

Again, each person should read over the questions for discussion provided. Then you should proceed through them as a group, discussing each in turn and writing your answer to the last one. If you wish to deal with any very briefly or to go into any at length, feel free to do so. They are intended to aid you in exploring the effect of *influence* or *decision-making* on your group. Use any procedure that you think best for achieving this goal.

1. Which people seem to have the most influence in the group? That is, when they talk others seem to listen and usually go along with them?
2. Have there been any shifts in influence from person to person? What has caused these changes to occur? Has there been rivalry for influence? How have these struggles, if any, been resolved?
3. How have most decisions been made in your group? Has everyone been satisfied with what you've done, or does one person generally impose his or her will on the rest? Does the majority push its approach through over the objections of the others? Have there been attempts to get everyone in on planning each activity? Have any individuals felt they made contributions which were ignored by the others?
4. How have people helped the group along by performing important functions, such as:
   a. Asking others for suggestions as to the best way to proceed or to tackle a problem?
   b. Summarizing or tying together several different comments?
   c. Keeping the group on target, rather than going off on tangents or jumping around from idea to idea?
   d. Including others in the discussion by asking for their opinion?
5. How have the influence and decision-making patterns of your group affected the two aspects of a successful group (enjoyment of the experience and quality of the group's work)? Each individual should write an answer to this question on this sheet as a record of what was learned from this discussion period.

Envelope #9

The following is an example of a limited but enjoyable form of creativity, creating new words to a familiar tune. After looking over this example, use whatever method you would like to create one verse to this or any other familiar song on the theme of "being a student today."

111

THE TEACHER'S LAMENT[1]
(to the tune of "Sixteen Tons," a folk song)

Some people say
a teacher's made out of steel
Her mind can think
but her body can't feel
iron and steel and hickory tea
frowns and gripes
from nine to three

I got eighty-four kids
and forty-two seats
Sixty are talking
while twenty-four sleep
I can hardly get 'em all
through the classroom door
And if I don't watch out
they'll give me twenty-four more

You teach six full hours
and what do you get?
Another day older
and deeper in debt
You pay your dues
in this and that
Then for twenty-nine days
your bill-fold's flat

You teach six full hours
to eighty-four brats
And all of them yelling
like dogs and cats
They're cutting on the seats
and writing on the walls
Hugging and kissing
in the upstairs halls

I woke one morning
it was cloudy and cool
I picked up my register
and started for school
I wrote eighty-four names
on the home-room roll
and the principal said
"Well, bless my soul"

The last bell rings
and I start for the door
My head is ringing
And my feet are sore
I taught six full hours
my day is made
But I still have
three hundred papers to grade

You teach six full hours
and what do you get?
Cuts and bruises
and dirt and sweat
I got two black eyes
and can hardly walk
When I turned my back
then came the chalk

You teach six full hours
and what do you get?
Another day older
and deeper in debt
I'll go to St. Peter
but I just can't stay
I gotta come back
to the P.T.A.

Envelope #10

This discussion period is devoted to considering what *norms* exist in your group, i.e., what is accepted, rejected, and avoided.

Once again, distribute copies of these questions and read them over. Then proceed to discuss those that seem most interesting and relevant to your group.

[1] Reprinted with permission from *Songs of Work and Protest* by Edith Fowke and Joe Glazer (New York: Dover Press, 1973).

Unspoken standards or ground rules usually develop in a group and influence what is said and done. These govern what *should* or *should not* occur. Some of these norms help the group and others are hindrances. It can be worthwhile to bring these out into the open. To do so in your group, consider the following questions:

1. Have group members been overly nice or polite to each other? Are only positive feelings expressed? Do members agree with each other too readily?
2. Do members feel free to question, challenge, or probe others occasionally? Do some people feel puzzled about others' behavior yet hesitate to ask them about it?
3. Are all feelings being experienced also being expressed, e.g., has there been any expressed or withheld anger, irritation, or frustration? any warmth or affection? any enthusiasm or excitement? any boredom? any hurt feelings or sadness? any competitiveness? If so, when expressed how have these been received? Have they been criticized or welcomed, or shades in between? If these feelings have been withheld, what made those individuals repress them?
4. How have the norms or unspoken rules about what is OK and what is not OK affected the two aspects of a successful group (*enjoyment* of the experience and the *quality* of the group's work)? Each individual should write an answer as a record of what was learned from this discussion period.

Envelope #11

This is a simple yet challenging exercise in creativity. Operating as a group, using whatever materials you can come up with from your pockets, bags, books, or anything else you have handy, make a sculpture or a structure which expresses your feelings about the creative process in your group. (This may seem strange at first, but can become fascinating after you get into it.) Take fifteen minutes to complete. At the end of that time someone in your group should be ready to explain what you have created to the rest of the class.

Envelope #12

Distribute a copy of this sheet to each person.

Try to spread out in the center of your group all the work you have done so far in this whole series of group creativity tasks. Look them over and recall what occurred and what you learned from each one.

Then each person should write on the sheet a statement summarizing the overall meaning these activities and discussions have had for him or her. Try to be frank and thorough. Some moments probably have been insightful and fun; others probably were confusing, frustrating, or boring. We can learn from all kinds of experiences; sometimes we get as much from negative ones as from those that are positive. Try to clarify why you reacted as you did in each instance and to make each one into a learning experience

113

by jotting down an insight into creativity, group interaction, or creative synthesis that emerges as an explanation for what occurred. After these have been completed, go around your group, asking each person to share a part (or all) of what he or she has written. Thus, you will benefit from others' thinking as well as your own.

(NOTE: At the end of each class period, or after the whole sequence of tasks is completed, an opportunity might be provided for reports from each group on what each did and what each learned. This will serve several purposes. It provides clear feedback on how this unit has been perceived. It satisfies each group's curiosity about what has been going on elsewhere in the room. Finally, groups that are operating productively can provide encouragement to others which may be having some difficulty.)

VI

The rationale and procedures described in this chapter have been valuable assets for me in teaching group communication at the high school and college undergraduate level. The specific tasks detailed here are about my fifth revision of this same basic procedure. I am certain this version will not be my last. I expect to continue revising and refining it each time. Nor should this be adopted by any reader without adaptations specific to his or her students and his or her beliefs about teaching.

Hopefully, I have raised some fresh propositions for readers to consider, encouraged them to include an additional tool in their instructional repertoire, and provided an incentive for employing their own creativity in introducing this area of study in their classrooms.

Note

I began this volume by speculating about how my own professors of twenty years ago would view the content of current offerings in interpersonal communication. They would, I assumed, be quite surprised at the new areas being addressed within this discipline. I suspect their eyes would widen still farther at the methods now in use. Then, formal public discussions were the primary classroom activity for units on interpersonal communication. Now, structured exercises of all sorts are being employed to illustrate communication principles that apply to informal everyday interaction.

In fact, this field has helped to pioneer a variety of instructional methodologies that depart dramatically from the norm throughout academia. In most classrooms today, the prevailing mode is still limited to lectures, class-wide discussions, and student reports. A visitor to an interpersonal communication classroom, however, might see chairs drawn into small, animated discussion groups, simulations of organizational life being enacted, competitive games being played, nonverbal messages being exchanged, etc. Indeed, these innovations range so far from the stodgy patterns being continued in other disciplines that in many institutions concerted efforts must be made to explain and justify their academic rationale to dubious colleagues.

The primary stimulus for this experimentation with innovative methodologies may be the fact that few other disciplines are working with material so readily available to classroom manipulation. Every student has a lifetime of experience with interpersonal communication situations which can be recalled for classroom discussion and analysis. Experiences which all students have in common can be generated at the behest of the classroom teacher through structured exercises that involve interaction. Other disciplines must rely on textbooks to confront students with the data to be examined. These two rich sources of sample events allow for many avenues of response as well.

In the following part, three still largely untried approaches to addressing interpersonal communication are proposed. The first, dealing with introspection, suggests a means for analyzing experiences that have already been completed in the lives of students — before they ever entered the classroom. The second, dealing with the encounter group, describes how experiences spontaneously generated within the classroom can be used to heighten students' awareness and competency in developing greater interpersonal intimacy. The last, dealing with dyadic episodes, describes how experiences can be developed that extend classroom learnings to times and places that more closely approximate the arenas in which students actually carry out their interpersonal contacts. In each of these ways the array of choices currently available to the teacher of interpersonal communication is stretched still farther.

CHAPTER 7

Introspection:
An Approach to Individualizing
Communication Instruction

I

Inherent in the encounter between students and the discipline of communication are several characteristics which imply how it should (and should not) be taught. A student enters a class in interpersonal communication carrying deeply embedded attitudes and habits developed during a lifetime of participation in the process to be studied. In fact, each student has a *unique* life history. No two people grow up under identical conditions. Every individual has contacted a network of significant people who have shaped his or her thinking and behavior when relating to others.

In addition, at the moment of taking the class, each student has specific relationships to which he or she would like to apply what is being learned. To be maximally meaningful, new awarenesses must be transferable to one's current position vis-à-vis family, friends, and others with whom one relates. Similarly, the specific personal and professional future each student foresees can have distinct implications for his or her communication needs.

In sum, all students have different pasts, presents, and anticipated futures which markedly influence how they will perceive and react to their experiences in studying interpersonal communication. Such predispositions place this field of study in sharp contrast to virtually all others in the educational spectrum. Usually, instructors of a foreign language, science, history, mathematics, or literature can assume that students have never been exposed to the ideas they will be presenting, that all students need to learn a common corpus of material, and that they will apply their learnings in a predictable social context.

Teaching in interpersonal communication that attempts to greatly redirect a student's daily used, lifelong patterns, that ignores his or her past and current phenomenal world, that seeks change where no need for it is felt is doomed to failure. Only an intensely *individualized* approach is appropriately suited to this discipline.

The need for individualization may account for the current movement toward using classroom group experiences incorporating individual feedback. Nevertheless, such exercises still leave the student subject to the norms of the classroom peer group or the observation form used. Informal papers encouraging students to react personally to course ideas are a step closer to individuation of learning, although they are usually designed unsystematically and bring scattered, superficial responses. My intent is to propose a more comprehensive approach to bring the reservoir of students' preconceptions to bear on their learning. This approach suggests procedures for including self-awareness or introspective experiences in communication instruction.

II

The literature dealing with interpersonal relations that now accounts for individual differences most thoroughly is in the realm of counseling and psychotherapy. The professional in these fields is expected to consider each client individually, to help him/her explore his or her current life situation, the path that led to it, and how greater satisfaction can be attained in personal relationships. These aims are closely related to the goals of instruction in interpersonal communication. Many theoretical frameworks, each stressing a different perspective of this process, exist to guide counselor-client dialogue. Almost all have some, as yet indefinite, degree of effectiveness. Most counselors now employ a variety of approaches, selecting the one (or more) which seems most suitable in each case.

Recently it has been found that when counselees or students are armed with these techniques themselves, self-directed growth can occur. This process has been particularly effective with applications to human relations training. When given the interventions usually employed in such workshops in packaged form, patients and students have gained as much as others in professionally-led groups.[1, 2] Much the same can be done to individualize instruction in interpersonal communication.

I have employed this approach by accompanying each lecture-discussion unit in my course (on interpersonal communication) with a handout that poses a series of questions designed to encourage student introspection. Students respond *only* to those questions with which they feel comfortable and motivated to answer, thus maximizing personal relevance and minimizing the danger of intruding into vulnerable areas.

One might be concerned that such questions, drawn from the repertoire of highly-trained professionals, might prove too potent or explosive for students to handle on their own. This concern merits consideration and ultimately, since this issue cannot be fully resolved through objective measures, each instructor should use only those he or she feels confident about. Keep in mind that the greatest danger to psychological health comes from pressures unwillingly and inappropriately inflicted on a vulnerable individual. When group pressure and leader influence are not present, when students can choose to deal only with questions that seem to be of value to them, with which they feel comfortable and motivated to answer, their safety is most effectively assured. Compare such freedom with front-of-the-room exposure demanded of anxious or reticent students in a public speaking class, and the relative danger in this process is extremely low, while the rewards are potentially great.

A paradigm for such a series of questions, each based on a theory of counseling or psychotherapy, appears in section IV. At the beginning of the semester, before considering any of the unit-specific questions, students are asked to take some overall perspectives to enhance the effectiveness of their subsequent introspective explorations. These are summarized in the following section.

III

The student's introspection is pointed in three general directions: toward the past, at the present, and into the future. Each orientation is broadly established by an initial experience which provides a foundation for more specific subsequent examination.

The student gains a perspective of the *past* by drawing a lifeline. One begins simply by drawing a line across a blank page and labeling one end "birth" and the other "now." He or she is then asked to divide the line into segments, cutting the line each time a major period ended or he or she became involved in a new context. For example, each new residence, school, job, or major friendship, each birth, death, or marital change which affected him or her would be entered. Finally, he or she lists the contexts, the people most significant in each setting, the major tasks each involved, and the degree of success or happiness felt in each. This overview of one's life provides a reference which can be consulted when contemplating past influences on current behavior.

Present opportunities and issues are reviewed by drawing a "role-network." This consists of a large circle surrounded by several smaller ones, like a sun circled by planets. The large circle is oneself; the smaller ones are the people with whom one relates most often or who are most important at this time in one's life. The student identifies the role assumed towards each person, and vice versa (e.g., father-son, husband-wife), the major trans-actions each relationship involves (e.g., socializing, decision-making, per-sonal sharing), the ways in which each relationship currently is satisfying and how each might be improved. This summary of his or her current communication field provides the student with a reference for con-templating how the course material can be applied in his or her life at present.

The *future* anticipated is summarized in a "weekly context" chart which has the headings of a weekly appointment page — the days of the week listed across the top and the periods of the day listed down the left-hand side. The student imagines how time slots will be filled, and down the center lists the contexts and people with whom he or she expects to be interacting during a typical week one month, one year, and five years into the future (e.g., teaching a class of high school students, making decisions with a spouse). These future opportunities for communication, along with the dissatisfactions identified in current relationships, provide an individualized set of goals or target situations for future application of the instruction to be received in interpersonal communication.

These personalized overviews of the students' past, present, and future in communication are further detailed and employed regularly throughout the semester as they consider all units in the curriculum and, through introspection, relate them to their own lives.

IV

The entries in this section provide basic models for devising introspective questions to supplement each unit of study in a course in interpersonal communication. The term *process* X is used where the specific topic or unit title would be inserted. Some of the topics to which I have applied these questions in my own teaching include: initiating relationships, group decision-making, conflict resolution, self-disclosure, the helping relationship, informing others, persuading others, group creativity, support and confrontation, leadership and conformity, etc.

The questions here are articulated as succinctly as possible. They are intended to serve as skeletal forms which should then be elaborated or fleshed out in order to best suit the topic and student group for which they are being used.

Each question is introduced with a brief rationale, offered merely as a reminder for those already familiar with that approach, and a reference for further investigation of the theoretical premises for those not familiar with them.

A. Influences of the Past

1. Albert Bandura[3] found that children are highly influenced by the adult models to which they have been exposed, particularly their parents. People often unconsciously adopt parental communication styles and carry them into their own adult lives. Consequently, it might prove insightful to ask:

    How did your parents or others in your family generally handle *process* X? Can you identify any similarities between their behavior and your own?

2. Freudian therapy[4] is based on the process of "transference" wherein the therapist is treated as a parent figure or someone else with whom the patient has an unresolved relationship. An individual's reactions to others is often influenced by their resemblance to people encountered earlier in life. It can be insightful, therefore, to ask:

    Examine your role network and identify the people with whom you have difficulty when dealing with *process* X. Do any of them remind you of someone with whom you shared a similar experience earlier in your life? If so, how are the relationships similar, and how are they different?

3. Phillips[5] found that college students who were particularly shy or reticent could recall with much more vivid detail embarrassing or ineffectual speaking situations from their early childhood than could more outgoing students. This finding suggests that a striking or traumatic negative experience can influence one's attitude toward similar experiences years later. It might, therefore, be insightful to ask:

> Can you recall an experience involving *process* X that was keenly embarrassing or frustrating? What about it made it so? As you think about engaging in *process* X, to what extent do you believe memories of that past experience affect your current attitude toward it?

4. One of the practices in "psychosynthesis" developed by Roberto Assagioli[6] is the training of will power. A technique that he employs is encouraging vivid, detailed recall of past experiences in which one willfully and successfully completed acts comparable to ones now appearing desirable. To put this practice to use, one might ask the student to:

> Identify an experience you have had using *process* X that was particularly satisfying or rewarding to you. Recall what *you* did to bring it about, being as specific or detailed as possible in delineating the steps you took. List them in chronological order, if you can, and feel no qualms about boasting or affirming proudly your contribution to making that experience a successful one. For example, you might begin each statement with "I _____" and then continue by spelling out one dimension of your positive behavior.

5. There is greater interest now than ever before in teaching communication skills at earlier levels of schooling.[7] Many students may already have had some formal training in the process to be taught. It might be wise to have them recall this by asking the following question:

> Have you ever learned about *process* X in school, read about it in a book, or in any other way had some formal instruction in how to deal with situations like these? If so, what did you learn that sticks in your mind today?

6. Eric Berne[8] highlighted the lingering role of parental admonitions in determining present-day behavior. He suggested that at times one's interaction is guided by "old tapes" or parents' homilies about "good" behavior or what "should" be done. This postulate suggests the question:

> How would your parents have advised you to behave when doing

X? Would their advice be different for dealing with the specific people in your role network? To what extent do you strive to live up to this advice?

7. Carl Jung[9] subdivided individual responses into the "persona" (the superficial social mask of the individual presented to others in social relationships) and the "ego" (a deeper part of the psyche which is reflective of personal experiences and is partly conscious and partly unconscious). When these two differ a person often experiences disharmony and frustration. Similarly, Andrew Salter[10] believes that people experience difficulty when they inhibit their emotions and greater effectiveness when they express them. One's inhibitions are learned, so he encourages relearning of expressiveness. He rewards feeling talk, physical expression of feelings, and spontaneous action. His "conditioned reflex therapy" is simply reinforcement of spontaneous, emotional responses. This orientation suggests the following line of questioning:

> In our desire to get along with others, at times we don't fully reveal or act in accord with what we really think or feel. Can you recall instances, when engaging in *process* X, when your social self or mask differed markedly from your inner or real self? If so, identify the people or conditions at those times which influenced your inhibition. Imagine what might have happened and how you would have felt if you had been more fully open and honest. Consider whether those same influences exist currently. What implications, if any, does this exploration have for your future growth goals?

B. Exploring the Present

1. Carl Rogers[11] stresses the value of the counselor's genuine, emphatic, supportive interaction with the client for enhancing self-awareness and feelings of self-worth. Since we are dealing with an individual's solitary introspection, a technique developed by George Kelly[12] called "self-characterization" allows for an imagined helping relationship of the type advocated by Rogers. His approach, adapted a bit for the purpose of communication instruction, calls for the student to:

> Write a description of yourself describing what you think, feel, and do during the *process* of X, just as if you were the principal character in a play. Write it as it might be written by a friend who knows you very well, who cares about you, who likes and respects you, and who is honest and open about what he or she says. Be sure to write it in the third person. For example, start out by saying, "He or she is _____." Then review this sketch and underline the statements which are of greatest significance for guiding your future personal growth in this process.

2. The methodologies of meditation[13] and psychoanalysis[14] encourage unrestricted awareness of whatever comes to mind. Both suggest

that one monitor or register ongoing thoughts for a period of time without judgment. The former advocates that this process be done internally in order to enhance inner peace. The latter employs verbalizing, called "free association," to enhance self-awareness. This process can be done by simply asking the student to:

> Begin with the phrase *process* X, and then think aloud on paper, writing whatever comes to mind, trying not to censor anything except to return to this theme when you wander from it. Do this for ten minutes without lifting your pencil from the paper. Then look back over what you have written and underline what seems most significant to you.

3. E. G. Williamson states that the counselor helps "the individual appraise himself *in comparison with external requirements,* whether they be school, vocational, or societal. Thus we help him to measure himself against the requirements of the external society." [15] Thus, the following question is implied:

> Review your current context chart. In which situations do opportunities arise to use X? Briefly assess your ability to employ X to your own satisfaction in each context. What differences exist between the contexts in which you feel confident and those in which you are less effective?

4. Albert Ellis[16] believes that the counselor must identify the beliefs or generalizations which guide a client's evaluation of his/her experiences. He believes that that many people, after engaging in an interpersonal encounter, evaluate the interaction by irrational, impossible standards that balloon feelings of self-denigration. He encourages clients to judge themselves more kindly, more realistically.

> By what criterion or standard do you judge whether or not you have done *process* X to your satisfaction? In other words, what would have to happen for an incident in which this process was involved to be successful? What would make you feel it was a failure? We often set unrealistically high standards for ourselves, making frustration likely. Review your evaluation criteria for this possibility, perhaps by considering whether you would want a best friend to live up to them. If they seem too demanding, revise them until they seem within the realm of possibility.

5. Thomas and Biddle[17] stress the influence of one's role vis-à-vis others on how they interact. Each social role comes laden with expectations or norms that make many behaviors within that role relatively predictable. A student's awareness of behavior in regard to a particular communication process might be clarified if he/she examined what his/her and the other's roles are:

> Look over your role network and consider how (if at all) the way you deal with *process* X differs with each person. Then consider how your role and those of other people (e.g., friend, sibling, student) affect your interaction.

6. Recently, much attention has been given to the way our society's racial[18] and sex-role[19] stereotypes shape individual behavior. To explore the possible influence of those forces on your students, it might prove fruitful to ask:

> To what extent do you believe that your race or ethnic status (being white, Jewish, Italian, Black, Indian, Puerto Rican, etc.) has influenced how you behave in situations involving *process X*? By examining your role network, do you recall any differences in your interaction when involved with someone of your own racial or ethnic group from what your experience is like with a member of another group? To what extent do you believe your sex has influenced how you behave when involved in *process* X with members of the opposite sex?

7. Joseph Shorr[20] encourages his clients' use of imagination for insights into their phenomenological worlds. He uses a technique, called "the most-or-least method," to help them sharpen their awareness of their attitudes and values. Some examples of how it might be adapted are:

> What is the worst thing that could happen to you in *process* X? What is the best thing someone could say about your employment of *process* X?

8. The "sentence completion" method is a widely used and highly regarded projective technique.[21] It requires response to a line of inquiry that can quickly identify an individual's preconceptions and goals in that area. Some potential applications of this device might be:

> If I were asked how to engage in *process* X effectively, I'd answer
>
> _____.
>
> A question I would like to ask an expert in *process* X is _____.

9. Harry Garner[22] has developed what he calls "confrontation problem-solving therapy," in which he stridently challenges the existing mental set of a client who is experiencing difficulty with a statement that usually reminds the client of his or her potential for more effective functioning. Then he *always* asks: "What do you think or feel about what I told you?" This encourages reflection in a new, less negative, often productive direction. Students might do the same if asked:

> Suppose someone who is wise and caring and who knows you well were to tell you, "You can do *process* X, stop believing that you can't." What would you think or feel about what you were told?

C. Affecting the Future

1. Victor Frankl emphasizes the significance of long-range hope or meaning in enhancing the determination and effectiveness with which one deals with current struggles in life. He stresses that clients clarify what they most want to accomplish, i.e., they identify the tasks that would give meaning and value to their lives. He states that these

"values do not drive a man; they do not *push* him, but rather *pull* him." [23] It might be helpful, therefore, for students to clarify how a process in communication fits into their personal goals by considering:

> If, after you die, someone were to write an obituary describing who you were and what you did in the time of your life, and were to describe you as you would like to be, what are some accomplishments that you would want to see included? How, if at all, might increased skill or use of *process* X help you to realize these accomplishments?

2. Counselors who employ behavior modification[24] suggest that long-range, vaguely expressed goals can be less effective in achieving change than short-term objectives that can be objectively evaluated. These provide quick and frequent checkpoints and opportunities for reinforcement. Consequently, the student might be asked:

> Examine your weekly context chart(s) for the near future and decide upon a time and place when you might employ *process* X in a new or more effective way. Describe in as much detail as you can what you will do, with whom, when, and where. Try also to state what would have to happen for you to consider this action to have been successful.

3. Raths, Harmin, and Simon[25] believe that people operate most effectively when they are clear about the values underlying their behavior. One way that they assist value clarification is to ask students to consider the alternatives to their decisions. When individuals have made a choice after freely contemplating all their options, they believe the decision is more likely to be satisfying.

> Another step in evaluating your goal(s) is to consider what other choices you could have made. People often make decisions without adequately assessing and choosing among their available options. Try to list some other possible goals that you could have chosen, and rank their desirability along with the choice you have already made. Is your first choice still the preferred one?

4. Karen Horney[26] stressed the danger of attempting to live up to too idealized a self-image. She encouraged her clients to realistically face and accept their actual selves before attempting to achieve personal growth. The following activity might prove helpful for students:

> Consider whether the goal(s) you have set for yourself are realistically attainable. It can be frustrating to pursue idealistic, but inappropriate, goals. Rate this goal on a scale of one to ten in terms of the likelihood that you will achieve it (one being very unlikely, ten being very likely). If your rating is below seven, perhaps you should rephrase it in a more modest way.

5. Frederick Perls[27] stressed that human behavior often follows an internal dialogue between two poles of the self, which he called the

top dog and the underdog. The former advocates an ideal behavior, the latter brings up excuses or reasons for avoiding it. He encouraged his clients to externalize this dialogue, hopefully thereby integrating both parts of themselves and feeling more centered, less conflicted about their experiences.

This process might be encouraged through the suggestion:

If you experience a desire to achieve your goal *and* some hesitation or resistance to pursuing it, imagine that each impulse has a voice of its own and write a dialogue in which these two parts or voices within you speak to each other, hopefully, until some resolution is reached.

6. In the reality therapy of William Glasser[28] clients are expected to identify what they want, to agree to do what is necessary in order to attain their goals, and to responsibly carry out the necessary steps until the job is completed satisfactorily. By encouraging them to take responsibility for themselves and to do so successfully, he is helping them to feel more capable and to bring more of their lives under their own control, thus empowering them to live more effectively. Students can practice this process with this exercise:

Identify the time or date by which you would like to achieve your goal. Also, describe what you will need to do in order to bring it about. Write this up as a contract with yourself, e.g., "By date X, I will _____." Then try to live up to that commitment. (If you do not, it means that you still had unrealistic expectations and may need to write another contract that is more appropriate.)

7. Ayllon and Azrin[29] change behavior by using a token economy. This is based on the notion that people do whatever gets them what they want (rewards). A student can set up a personal reward system through introspection.

If you were to carry out this step, what reward(s) would it bring? In what way might you plan a reward for yourself that would encourage you even more to carry it out?

8. J. L. Moreno[30] developed "psychodrama" in which individuals role-play the relationships in which they experience conflict. One technique used is "role reversal," in which the client plays the role of the other person in the relationship. This assists one in seeing the situation from the other's point of view, as well as in being more aware of the thoughts one believes the other has. This process can be approximated by asking the student to carry out the following activity:

Write the dialogue of the situation you would like to change as you suspect it will occur, i.e., use your imagination to predict what will happen and write it out. This script can provide clues as to where you believe problems might arise and, perhaps, ideas about how they might be overcome.

9. Everett Shostrom[31] believes that the feelings which underlie our

behavior must be brought to the surface and be openly acknowledged. A student might grow in awareness of the unspoken feeling-level beneath much interaction by performing this exercise:

> Review the dialogue you wrote earlier and try to guess the feeling each person might be experiencing when speaking (e.g., fear, anger, hurt, joy). Write these emotions in the margin next to the comments. Then consider how the situation might work out if these feelings were openly acknowledged.

V

Responses to these questions can be useful in a variety of ways. For students, they serve to heighten consciousness of the process being studied; they help to explain the sources of everyday behavior and the role each process plays in daily life; they suggest how the process is relevant to the future and how each person can take responsibility for putting into action what is learned in class. The responses would also be of interest to their peers. Students are usually eager to compare their answers with those of others in group discussion. Finally, they can provide the teacher with insights into how the course material relates to the phenomenal world of the students. Although students should have the right to keep their responses private, some voluntary sharing with the teacher can suggest many specific examples and adaptations for use in making lecture material more immediately applicable to the particular student population.

These questions were intended only to provide raw material for further processing through the sensitivities and professional judgment of the communication instructor. Hopefully, they suggest ways to lay the foundation from which students can adapt a uniform text, lecture, or exercise to the contours of their unique existence. The instructor is an individual, too, with a personal history and already developed screening mechanisms which will be involved in selecting the questions that seem mmst appropriate and valuable for his or her curriculum. My experience makes me confident that such questions serve to markedly increase students' personal involvement and also to increase the rewards they reap from course work in communication.

CHAPTER 8

*The Encounter Group**

Suppose we sliced the tops off all the buildings in the United States and used a helicopter to hover and look down upon them. We would see people seated behind desks and machines in businesses, around kitchen tables and televisions, lying in hospital beds and jail cells, standing in elevators and in supermarket aisles. We would hear countless words of instruction, advice, persuasion, humor, reassurance, an innumerable variety of messages. Across the length and breadth of the land, however, a few hundred scenes similar in both appearance and dialogue would recur in the pattern that is the focus of this chapter.

Our pattern would usually be found in a large institutional cluster of buildings, such as a university, or in an isolated rural retreat, perhaps on the California coast. From high above we would see a dozen or more people in a circle seated at ease in comfortable chairs or sprawled on the floor. This group could be observed continuing for from two to twenty-four hours at a time. Depending on where we chose to descend for a closer examination, we might see homogeneous groups of students, co-workers, or members of the same profession. We might also see groups which seem to be deliberately mixed, including some with white people and members of a minority group, or adults and adolescents, or even a single group that maximized diversity by deliberately intermingling people of various ages, races, sexes, and vocations.

As we hover close enough to see and hear what each person is doing and saying, the special nature of this circle of communicators would be vividly revealed. The faces and bodies of the participants might seem unusually intent on whoever is speaking, and the speaker's feelings might be easily inferred from observation. The urgent tone of the voices would offer a clue to the emotional climate in the group, as would sentences beginning with "I feel . . .," "What's your reaction to . . .?" and "Let's work this through. . . ."

---

* This chapter was co-authored by H. Keith McConnell, Ph.D. and is printed with permission.

Had we attempted this fantasy trip over Athens 2,500 years ago we might have seen a similar group surrounding Socrates. In Jerusalem over 1,900 years ago such a group might have included early followers of Jesus Christ. During the Middle Ages Benedictine and Trappist monks held group sessions for personal growth. Early in this century, an American physician named Joseph Pratt helped in the cure of tuberculosis patients by assembling them into a modified version of an encounter group.

The emergence of the encounter group as we know it today, however, can be traced to a chance occurrence on the campus of the State Teachers College in New Britain, Connecticut, during the summer of 1946. A group of community leaders was conferring about the implementation of a new Fair Employment Practices Act. Their approach was to discuss their hometown problems in racial discrimination within small groups. Associated with this conference was a team of observers undertaking some research on group dynamics. Their role was to record the interaction within each discussion group. Every evening the observers met to pool their notes on what they had seen. For example, an observer might have noted what the group leader did, who changed the subject, what conflicts occurred, how decisions were made, etc. A few participants began to attend these note-sharing sessions. When the time came for their own group's behavior to be described and analyzed, they became extremely interested and eager to interject comments on how they saw what had occurred. These conversations were lively and felt to be highly profitable. Soon all the participants were attending these sessions and taking part. What had started as brief work meetings often stretched on for hours and became the forerunner of today's encounter group.

The next year this team of researchers, including Kurt Lewin, Ronald Lippitt, Kenneth Benne, Leland Bradford and others, founded the National Training Laboratories (NTL) which has since offered hundreds of workshops for people from all fields. The basic core of these workshops is the dialogue about how people are reacting to what actually goes on within the group itself. The immediacy and honesty of a good encounter group was found to be so useful and satisfying that these groups spread rapidly from coast to coast and were incorporated into organizations such as businesses, schools, and mental health facilities.

The most newsworthy medium for the encounter group has come to be the "growth" center whose business it is to conduct encounter groups for the public at large. This phenomenon of organized personal develop-ment is of significant proportions. One pioneer in this area, Esalen Insti-tute, reported that in 1976 almost 2,500 persons attended the various work-shops and intense group experiences they offered. Similar centers exist in virtually every metropolitan area and major university town in the United States.

The encounter group is but one of several vehicles which have emerged in the recent dramatic upsurge of activity subsumed by the term *humanism*. Those working in this field hope to revitalize concern for humanity, help people to more fully develop their potential, and change the focus of our society to its most vital part—the human element. In this age of mass technology and dehumanization, the need for a renewed appreciation of the individual has become critical. The humanist believes that there is a process of becoming and developing which is natural yet unique for everyone. The encounter group is a potent means to aid in this process and to help meet this need.

The focus of most formal education is on the cognitive grasp of subject matter. Unfortunately, this attempt to maximize knowledge, to accumulate facts, and to develop our powers of reason and logic has resulted in neglecting a significant portion of our capacity to function meaningfully. Psychologists such as Maslow (1968) have argued that within most individuals there lies an array of talents waiting to be tapped, especially those which depend on spontaneity, emotional expression. The encounter group and other related forms of experiential learning aim to realize human potential more fully.

To help understand what an encounter group is supposed to be, consider the following statement published by Esalen Institute (1972):

> The ground rules of encounter are that participants be open and honest in a group setting, that they avoid mere theorizing and instead talk about their feelings and perceptions. There is often an emphasis on eliciting emotions which lead to positive or negative confrontations rather than away from them. The focus of encounter is to explore interpersonal relations.

But why does an open, candid conversation prove so attractive to so many people? Clearly, it must provide an opportunity which does not normally exist in their everyday lives. A cursory review of an individual's growth reveals how such a vacuum forms. Most small children freely express whatever they feel using sounds, words, and their bodies. When children are angry, happy, sad, or hurt their parents know it. Their voices and faces vividly portray their states of mind. Particular feelings, however, upset some parents, and they demand that their children suppress them. Let's take one example. Some parents believe that children should not be assertive or angry. They reprimand a complaining or demanding child with admonitions like "Don't talk back," or "Be respectful," or "If it's not nice, don't say it." That child soon learns not to disagree. Unwelcome thoughts and feelings are suppressed. Soon the child's public personality is limited to agreeable, cordial comments. He or she finds it almost painful to say no, to assert a point of view in opposition to others, or to take a position of leadership. This dimension of his or her potential has been stifled, at least overtly. Despite this restriction, no one can avoid feeling angry, annoyed, or want to assert his or her will over others throughout a lifetime. Usually when these feelings are aroused, they are repressed, at least until they can be held in no longer, when an explosive "get-it-off-my-chest" outburst occurs. In an encounter group the full spectrum of feelings is encouraged and accepted. In this climate one need not repress spontaneous reactions. One can experiment with expressing whatever is felt, with being open and honest. One learns how to deal with others' reactions to these feelings.

Thereby, a new dimension of individual potential is actualized, one is free to be more fully oneself, and the energy wasted on repression can be put into healthier channels. The popularity of encounter groups attests to the widespread need for this comprehensive degree of openness.

How do encounter groups do their work? To explore this question, let us conjure up two very imaginary participants and follow their initial interaction in an encounter group. One, whom we'll call Sandpaper, is an aggressive, impatient businessman. The other, Cotton, is a shy, reticent student. Their entire group of perhaps 12 people and a trainer meets in an informal setting with people sitting in a circle. At the beginning or soon after, there being no agenda imposed by the leader, the group finds it must determine its own direction. Sandpaper takes the lead in proposing an activity: everyone will introduce himself or herself by giving his or her name, life history, profession, etc. Some agree to this direction, others say it's a bad idea, and a few withdraw into passive noninvolvement. Cotton, being somewhat self-conscious, feels anxious about having a turn at being the focus of the group's attention. He sits with arms folded across his chest, looking annoyed. Sandpaper, sensing this resistance, asks him to begin. Cotton retorts, "Formal introductions are stupid!" The leader asks Cotton how he feels about introducing himself. He admits that he is self-conscious. Sandpaper interjects that he had not realized how his approach to opening meetings affected people like Cotton. The leader asks Sandpaper why he suggested giving introductions. After thinking for a minute, Sandpaper becomes aware that he feels uncomfortable with people whose backgrounds are unknown to him. The leader reflects an understanding of this need, yet instead of satisfying it urges Sandpaper to experiment with trying to get to know people without a title or social group affixed to them. In fact, Sandpaper is urged to share his immediate reactions to each group member, and then to check out their accuracy.

Within this brief synopsis of one hypothetical scene from an encounter group some basic procedures are evidenced. These will be explored. The reader might want to refer to the scene to recall each procedure as it is discussed. When Sandpaper took the initiative in the group, he revealed his customary approach to dealing with people — actively organizing their behavior. The others' responses to him provided clues to how they generally interact. Thus, *as people respond in a group they provide data about their typical communication style. These shared experiences can then be discussed among them.* Moreover, when Sandpaper and Cotton expressed the feelings behind their words, deeper insight was gained. The others got to know them as people, and perhaps they themselves grew a bit in self-awareness. In encounter groups people are encouraged to state their feelings explicitly, instead of just acting on them. Thus, instead of being evasive, one might say, "I don't trust you," or instead of shouting, "You're wrong," one might give the feeling behind it as "Your opinion makes me angry." When *feelings are explicit* instead of implied, they can be better understood and possible problems can be better worked out.

As the group reacted to Sandpaper's initiative, it was *discussing its own shared experience* as opposed to giving introductions in which outside events were to be narrated. In encounter groups, people often ask, "What are your reactions to what we just did?" "What have we been doing together?" "This is how I have been feeling about our conversation," etc. Discussions about childhood influences or disturbing relationships with people not in the group are more appropriate for psychotherapy or counseling groups.

When Cotton withdrew into a closed position it was apparent that he had something on his mind. Sandpaper asked him to express it, to say with words what his body was hinting. In encounter groups people are urged to be *congruent*; the clues offered by their faces, hands, and bodies are picked up and pointed out so that they might feel confident to be fully open, both verbally and physically. In our scene the body expressed the true feeling. At other times only people's words, not their bodies, express their messages. In these cases they might be urged to put their message into a physical form as well. For example, people who care for each other might hug, people who are angry might wrestle. The goal of congruency is to produce clear, unambiguous messages, which often are more satisfying both to senders and to receivers.

When asking Cotton to express how he felt instead of just attacking Sandpaper's suggestion, the trainer wanted him *to own responsibility for his reaction.* To attack is to make the other defensive, thereby encouraging a battle rather than understanding. The statement "I feel hurt," for example, locates that reaction in the speaker, instead of saying, "You insulted me," which is blaming the other person. The former is an example of an individual owning his or her own feeling.

When asking Sandpaper to give his immediate reactions to the people in the group, the trainer was urging him to be *spontaneous*, to reveal to others (and perhaps even to himself) his opinions as he was forming them, instead of waiting until they were firmly fixed. Encounter group participants often are encouraged to talk about what they are experiencing in the *now*, to say what they are thinking or feeling as closely as possible to the moment it comes into awareness, instead of withholding or repressing reactions for fear of what others might think of them. The trainer was also asking Sandpaper to *risk*, to try out an approach to relating to others that was not heretofore part of his communication style. What people hesitate to do is often most valuable for them. It provides a step toward fulfillment of another dimension of their potential.

When Sandpaper shared his anxiety about dealing with people whose backgrounds are unknown to him, the trainer expressed an understanding of that feeling. This is an example of *reflective listening*, another important component of encounter groups. Too often, when people allow themselves to be open and honest about their feelings, they receive responses of criticism, kidding, or advice; or their expression of feeling is ignored. Consequently, they close up again. In encounter groups expressions of feeling ideally are received with complete acceptance and understanding, whether they be warm or hostile, so that the speaker does not regret having shared his or her inner, more vulnerable self. Sufficient time is taken for that feeling to be expressed fully, using verbal or physical means, or both,

132

until the speaker feels the sense of relief and satisfaction that comes with authentic self-expression. Of course, the effects or consequences of this self-expression on others are treated with the same patience and care.

The leader asked Sandpaper why he suggested that everyone introduce themselves because of a hunch that a personal need lay behind that suggestion. Quite often people report intuitions, suspicions, or vibrations sensed during the course of an encounter group, and they are encouraged to do so. This diagnostic sensitivity can provide valuable clues to what is on others' minds that isn't being expressed clearly. The person who uses this extrasensory awareness becomes alert to indications of the underlying dynamics between people that words cannot express. One's own daydreams or fantasies are also used to provide clues to fuller self-awareness.

Not all proponents of encounter groups advocate the same leadership approach or the same participant behaviors. The primary distinction is probably the degree of leader directiveness. On the one hand, the minimally directive encounter group leader (e.g., Rogers, 1967) develops a supportive climate in which individual participants are cautiously guided towards mutual trust and openness. On the other hand, the more directive encounter group leader (e.g., Schutz, 1972) provides a more structured and confrontive atmosphere in which participants are repeatedly challenged to take charge of their own behavior.

There is a variety of groups which share many of the goals of the traditional encounter group (if an encounter group can be said to be "traditional"). For example, Gestalt-oriented leaders, following the lead of Frederick Perls, stress speaking spontaneously, being aware of and reporting what is occurring at the immediate moment (in the *now*). In Daniel Casriel's groups the expression of feelings is paramount; in fact, participants are urged to scream their feelings until they are totally identified with them and the feelings are completely ventilated. Thomas Gordon works with parents to make them more responsive listeners to their children's feelings. Reality Therapy, developed by William Glasser, reminds participants that they are responsible for their own behavior and the consequences it produces. Bio-Energetic Therapy, developed by Alexander Lowen, emphasizes how the body experiences and expresses emotions and works toward mind-body integration (or congruency). In T(raining)-Groups, the facilitator focuses on the processes by which the group takes action and develops closeness. Marathon group leaders utilize an extended time period to allow the more personal concerns of the members to be brought up and worked through. Finally, Robert Assagioli's Psychosynthesis method stresses awareness of insights available through attentive perception of one's intituitions, fantasies, and daydreams.

Each of these approaches stresses an element which is part of the encounter experience, yet each is unique. Although much of the same authentic, growth-stimulating communication goes on in each, their distinct features are important for they provide a variety of ways to achieve personal growth, each more suited to some individuals than others.

The encounter group is based on the assumption that people working together in relative openness and honesty can influence each other to reach higher degrees of self-actualization and awareness. Such a function may be termed "therapeutic." In fact, the encounter group is sometimes said to be therapy for the "normal."

People attend encounter groups to learn. They may hope to learn more about themselves, about other people, or about how people relate to one another. The leader believes these goals will be achieved most effectively if the group members communicate openly and honestly. Therefore, behaviors are encouraged which will lead to close, trusting relationships among them. Having seen and tried those behaviors, as well as being aware of their impact, participants can then judge how useful the behaviors would be in their everyday lives. They have gained some new skills which they can apply whenever they believe them to be appropriate for the situations in which they find themselves.

To recapitulate, when faced with a situation in which they or others seem to be feeling something strongly, communicators trained in human relations should be able to shift the conversation so that people are speaking spontaneously, expressing their feelings explicitly, and helping others feel accepted. This will enable participants to be open about their feelings without regret, own responsibility for their feelings, try to be congruent (send both verbal and nonverbal messages which are the same), discuss and examine their shared experience, give each other useful feedback, express and respect their intuitions, and be willing to take the time needed for working the issues through. In a sense, these behaviors are strategies for good encounter groups and, as we've seen, for many other interpersonal situations.

The experience of interacting frankly and forthrightly has some delightful side effects. The first "symptom" is feeling closer, more intimate with others in the group. Friendship is a treasured relationship, largely defined by people feeling free to be most truly themselves with each other. In a group where the full range of feelings is acceptable, one finds oneself talking about responses usually shared only with those closest to one, if at all. Having been open about one's responses to the group, one is filled with the same feeling of close friendliness usually reserved for family and intimate friends.

An attempt to express more about personal feelings than is typically socially acceptable requires a risk. One must be prepared to bear the consequences, to deal with the receiver's reaction, whether hostile, hurt, or embarrassed. This risk causes tension. The body tightens to receive the response. Once that response is found to be bearable and the risk is proved worthwhile, a great feeling of relief sets in. Repressed feelings create physical tensions manifested as headaches, tight muscles, and stomach upset. Expressed feelings allow the body to return to a natural, relaxed state. Side effect two, therefore, is a pleasing degree of physical harmony.

Finally, one feels more confident about facing and coping successfully with the emotion-laden situations in everyday life. Some new and very useful skills for human relations have been learned. The participant can master situations in which he or she had heretofore felt helpless. What had seemed confusing, formidable, and frustrating before now seems manageable. One's sense of competence increases, creating an enhanced self-image.

All these side effects explain the feeling of being "high" often reported by participants in successful encounter groups. They combine to produce a state of euphoria, of joy. It is an almost child-like feeling, the result of having returned for a time to that state of spontaneous authenticity effortlessly unhampered by the restrictions of social etiquette.

Although the emphasis in this chapter is on the encounter group per se, it is also important to consider other situations which can be affected by the use or nonuse of the group behaviors we've been discussing. For the encounter group to be a relevant learning experience, its essential ingredients must have some application to less artificial, day-to-day realities. Consider, for example, a business setting in which a meeting of several department heads is in progress. For over two hours these individuals have been bogged down in attempts to work out the best solution to the company's current problems. The same facts appear to be available to all, but some participants are unfairly blocking out the others' points of view. If the chairperson of the meeting were aware of these perceptual biases, he or she would have a choice: to continue talking only about the content or topic at hand or to try to deal with some of the underlying feelings of those involved. In effect, the chairperson has a choice similar to that of the encounter group leader. Is it more productive to keep the feeling level submerged, or can something useful be gained by acknowledging and exchanging feelings when they exist and are affecting the ongoing business interaction?

In many cases business meetings bypass the feelings of their members on the grounds that this situation is not the place for feelings — "business shouldn't meddle in this area!" There may be some truth to this fear, for surely I am not suggesting that a business function like an encounter group. Such an extreme would be ludicrous; but let's consider a compromise. Suppose the chairperson had offered the conflicting members the chance to voice their feelings toward each other at that time or perhaps in a private get-together later. It seems likely that such an exchange could shed some light on the reasons behind the disruptive barriers in the meeting so that more productive interactions could be pursued. Thus, as in an encounter group, it may sometimes be of value to examine the effects of unexpressed feelings on the behaviors around us.

Most proponents of encounter groups believe it is important for individuals to explore new behaviors, to take some risks, and thereby broaden their perception of what alternatives are in fact available to them. In a number of educational settings today, the student-teacher relationship has increased in scope and deepened in intensity and interpersonal involvement. One of the reasons for this change is analogous to certain encounter group tactics. One of the problems with traditional models of education was and still is the strict role-casting assigned to the student and to the teacher. The student should listen, follow instructions, answer questions when asked, do homework, show respect for the teacher, etc.; the teacher should lecture, be all-knowing, give examinations, assign grades, etc. Given these types of behavioral definitions of the student-teacher relationship, a teacher takes a considerable risk in initiating a new pattern of interaction which changes their former roles. Consider, for example, the teacher who decides to introduce student self-evaluations as a part of the grading scheme. Such an individual is giving students more responsibility for their own learning and has thus initiated a new and perhaps more meaningful pattern of teacher-student interaction. The principle is the same as in the encounter group — to grow is to risk, to explore, and to expand individual responsibility.

Business and education can indeed gain by utilizing encounter group ideas. Situations abound in which people need the skills of leading, following, cooperating, and compromising — in essence, the skills of relating with others, of being skilled in interpersonal communications. The formal organization is not the only place however, where encounter group strategies can be of value. The family scene, the group of friends, and even the casual social setting are all potential arenas for personal and interpersonal growth.

All too often the members of a family do not take responsibility for their feelings for one another; instead, they fall back on habitual responses and behaviors. Imagine for example, the college-aged male lecturing a younger brother about the latter's choice of friends: "Quit hanging around with those guys or I'll do something about it; they're a bad bunch and you should stay away from them! " The message is clear. The older brother is threatening and trying to control the behavior of the younger brother. But is that really his message? Are his words consistent with his feelings? Not likely. It's a safe bet that he is actually feeling concern for his brother, a sincere caring for his welfare. Again there exists the encounter group parallel. The opportunity exists for these two brothers to engage in an interaction which deals more explicitly with the heart of the issue. The older brother can perpetuate the game, or he can own up to his feelings and perhaps open new paths of growth between them.

Similarly, the commonplace situation of a group of friends interacting presents the opportunity to broaden their interactions by using some encounter group tactics. How often do friends really talk about what's happening in the present and in the now? Imagine two couples discussing the apparent dishonesty of the men and women in the movie just seen. If, in fact, they are expressing what they are seeking in their own relationship, would it not be of value to speak more directly about it? With a little effort, they, too, might be able to open new doors, to experience the initial discomfort and subsequent growth which is so often reported in the laboratory situation of the encounter group.

Social situations can also be vehicles for more meaningful human interactions. The casual chitchat of a cocktail party is full of behavioral inconsistencies which may be effectively brought into the open and used to the benefit of all concerned. If an individual is voicing verbal agreement to what is being said while his or her body is simultaneously negating the opinion, it might be worthwhile to clarify this incongruency, e.g., "I sense by your facial expression that you aren't really as agreeable to the idea as you said you were." Of course you could ignore the inconsistency and continue with what may be a somewhat dishonest interaction. Clearly, in all of the above instances the encounter group option involves some risk to the initiator. The experience of the effects and results will determine how often the risk will be taken in the future.

People from the preceding social categories frequently include the encounter group mode of learning in their formal attempts to acquire certain skills. For example, many business organizations send their managers to human relations training programs which have considerable overlap with the procedures of encounter groups. Each year the NTL Institute conducts numerous such labs, and thousands of individuals go away more attuned to the intricacies of human potential, interpersonal relations, and group dynamics. Clearly, these companies must consider this kind of learning experience to be of value to them. The same is true for other walks of life—the university trying to meet the needs of its students with courses in sensitivity training or encounter, the church program trying to revitalize its congregation, and the married couple or family striving for fuller and more authentic relationships.

But does subsequent change really occur as a result of the encounter group experience? The place to look for an answer to such a question is the research literature in the area of human relations training and small group interaction. Although much research has been done, there is a lack of conclusive evidence based on hard or objective data, due chiefly to the problems inherent in measuring the many dimensions of personal change.

Nevertheless, some conclusions have been drawn about the effects of the human relations group experience. For example, House (1967) studied the outcomes of human relations laboratory training for supervisors, and reported that it may have had the intended effect of inducing more consideration for subordinates, less dependence on others, less demand for subservience from others, and better communication through more adequate and more objective listening. However, he did suggest that such an experience is not likely ideal for all organizations nor for all situations.

Other kinds of effects have been reported. Individuals' self-perceptions can change as a result of such group experiences (Campbell and Dunnette, 1968), and, in some cases, similar changes are reported by participants' friends or co-workers in the back-home situation (Dunnette, 1969). This latter study revealed an increase in the empathic skills of group members. Bunker (1965) also noted some on-the-job changes in performance after an intense group experience. He reported that participants were more open, tolerant, more aware of self and others, and generally more skilled in interpersonal situations.

McConnell (1971) studied two human relations laboratory programs and reported that there were differential effects both in the groups and on some of the self-descriptive measures which were taken. As well as noting the consequences of the labs, e.g., that self-report measures showed the participants to be more sensitive to feelings, and more authentic in their relationships, he found that the more flexible, tolerant, and independent participants got along better in the groups, suggesting that perhaps the intense group experience may have better results for some people. The extremely closed-minded or defensive person is likely to have a difficult time in an encounter group. It is an irony that individuals who experience the most trouble in such group situations are the very ones who could most benefit by the learning if it occurred. This supports one of the cautions sometimes heard about the encounter group — namely, what's good for some isn't necessarily good for all.

The reader interested in the kinds of precautions to consider in deciding about joining an encounter group might well read an article like Shostrom's "Let the Buyer Beware" (1969). This human potential psychologist makes no bones about the fact that one should show some care before leaping into an unknown commodity. He discusses issues like the legitimacy of the sponsoring organization, the qualifications of the leader, and the motivation of the participant.

Something with as much potential good as the encounter group is also likely to have some potential drawbacks. For example, if a group becomes too self-analytical or picky in analyzing their shared experiences, feelings can be blurted out which put the speaker or receiver into an awkward or embarrassing situation; people can be pressured into believing that only one dimension of feelings such as hostility or love can be acceptably expressed; certain physical expressions of feelings can upset some individuals' existing personal values, etc. Group pressure can be misused.

Once feelings have been dealt with openly and honestly, and participants feel comfortable and close with their groups, the communication experienced together may become increasingly personal. The caring which people feel for each other might lead to sharing their deepest concerns, which could, at times, bring to the surface issues that are beyond the scope of the group to handle.

A critical issue concerning encounter group leaders is the back-home environment of the participants. How is the learning which goes on during the group experience transferable to the individual's everyday life? In some instances, the prevailing norms of behavior at home, at the office, etc., conflict drastically with the behaviors and beliefs of the encounter group. Individuals who undergo a significant growth experience and a marked change in personal style may find themselves in an uncomfortable situation when they try to interact with their everyday associates. Such people must be cautioned that their experience was probably unique and that they must take a step at a time back home. Their friends and associates did not share their experience; therefore, they may have difficulty explaining what they've learned or what they went through. Participants generally find considerable bafflement and some resistance if they take on the role of proselytizer for the "new way" of living. More than once ex-encounter groupers have been rejected by former associates. Here again the leader's role is crucial. The skilled encounter group leader would devote some time to the problems of reentry and transfer, to sharing the experience with non-participants, and to applying what was learned to new situations.

Thus, the encounter group is basically a laboratory, a setting in which exploration and learning can take place. It is a miniature society in that numerous parallels to the outside world can be seen. Many of the dynamics which occur in the life of an encounter group are the same as those in the development and life of groups, organizations and societies in the real world. The basic ups and downs of the communication process are the same. The difference lies in the nature of the accepted norms of communication. The encounter group broadens the scope of what is communicated and how it is communicated.

CHAPTER 9

Communication Education Through Dyadic Interaction

We try to keep class enrollments low in my department to allow for personal interaction between students and instructors. Recently, budgetary limits have brought about pressure to increase class size. Responding dutifully, I attempted to develop a course in my area of instruction that could handle large numbers of students. My procedure was to offer lectures on each topic in the curriculum, and then to divide the class into groups of five or six for structured opportunities to experience, observe, and share feedback about the processes being examined.

This model is widely used, yet despite many efforts to improve it, my students still grumbled about the "artificiality" of the classroom setting and the structured exercises. They would say, "I can talk so much more freely and genuinely *outside* of class, with *one* other person, but in this group, being told what to do and seeing all the other groups doing the same thing, I feel fake and uncomfortable." Dropping in on each group as an onlooker-consultant, I had to admit that I felt the same way.

Taking my cue from exactly what so many students had said, I replaced some group exercises with one-to-one dyads, to be held after the class, wherever and whenever students preferred (within the week after each lecture session). To evaluate the impact of this change, I solicited students' reactions. (The learning to be gained through interaction was intended to be highly personalized and individualized, suggesting, therefore, a subjective self-report approach to evaluation.) On the instruments I devised, they reported more *enjoyment* and *learning* from the dyads than from other course experiences (lectures, readings, writing papers, and group interaction). Some of the major reasons given for this preference were similar to aspects of dyadic interaction reported in research done on this process. A summary of the results of this informal study follows with citations to related small group literature.

Students reported that the dyads:

1. Seemed more relevant to their daily lives — most of their newly forming significant relationships are also experienced dyadically, e.g., dating and marriage, roommates, job interviews, etc.[1]
2. Seemed a more potent, intimate, memorable context for interaction — with only one person reacting to them, students became more open; they experienced more closeness, more investment and energy in their interaction, and more concern for each other.[2]
3. Provided this kind of contact with fascinating people they would ordinarily never get to know — campus living and social groups are often spread far apart and friendships tend to cluster around those with similar major areas of study and leisure-time interests.[3]
4. Developed deeper sensitivity to others with these new contacts — the phenomenal words behind people's masks were seen, social stereotypes were shattered, almost always evolving to a more positive view of one's partner.[4]
5. Provoked new insights into self-awareness as well — feedback from a partner was most direct and real, and they found themselves relating in ways they hadn't tried before, thereby seeing untapped potential within themselves worth releasing.[5]
6. Allowed the processes of interaction to emerge more clearly — with only two people interacting, issues, conflicts, decisions couldn't be avoided; attribution of causality for what occurred could be made more clearly.[6]
7. Usually turned out to be far more absorbing and intense than expected — apathy seemed impossible to maintain, the limits of the traditional student dropped away, and intereaction often evolved from a hesitant start to a surprisingly potent contact.[7]

Having tried and evaluated this approach I could not fathom why it hadn't been given more attention in communication education literature.[8] Other approaches to human growth use this one-to-one mode, e.g., psychotherapy, music lessons, medical treatment, etc. To move from individual speech-making to small group interaction, thereby bypassing dyadic encounters as is the case in most speech programs, is to diminish greatly the potency of instruction in communication. The purpose of this chapter is to provide the framework by which a communication teacher can add this medium to his or her instructional repertoire.

To employ this approach with optimum effectiveness for learning, the instructor must make several key decisions. These include:

1. What tasks are suited for dyadic interaction?
2. How are students and tasks matched?
3. How are students matched with dyad partners?
4. Under what conditions should dyads be held?
5. How are learnings drawn from dyadic experiences?

Each will be examined in turn.

What Tasks Are Suited for Dyadic Interaction?

The *tasks* which students can undertake in dyads are almost as numerous as those encountered in everyday life. Man is a goal-seeking organism. When two people interact they usually are seeking some kind of control, payoff, or reward.[9] Often several objectives are sought simultaneously, although one objective usually influences the encoding and decoding processes predominantly. To achieve that objective successfully, specific strategies or skills have been found to be helpful. A review of the literature reveals that several kinds of *objectives* and the *skills* needed to achieve them have been identified. Those appearing most frequently are summarized here.

When two people initiate a relationship, *socializing* skills are used and exploration of mutual interests occurs;[10] when they must make a decision, *problem-solving* skills are needed;[11] when creative ideas are sought, *idea-generating* techniques such as brainstorming and synectics can be helpful;[12] when knowledge must be transmitted, *expositional* and *instructional* skills are of value;[13] when issues are debated, techniques of *persuasion* are employed;[14] when agreement must be reached, methods of *negotiation* and *conflict-resolution* are called upon; [15] when someone is experiencing a personal crisis, *helping* responses are most appropriate;[16] when a personal choice must be made, *value clarification* methods are put into play;[17] when a matching of personnel and position is required, *interviewing* techniques are employed;[18] when personal intimacy or authenticity is sought, *T-group* procedures are put into effect;[19] when one seeks to heighten consciousness of political, ethnic, or sexual influences, *confrontational, consciousness-raising questions* in each area are posed.[20]

Each of these objectives for the communication process has been the focus for a unit of study in a course. Each can be experienced in dyadic interaction.

Several major variables differentiate these areas of communication from one another. Some are inherent within the tasks and others are related to the students' prior experiences. One is the *locus of dialogue.* There are two basic perspectives from this view. In several of the communication processes the locus of dialogue is on *external* tasks, and in others the content deals with *internal* perceptions, attitudes, feelings, and values. Another way of conceptualizing this variable is that in some cases the criteria for judging the success of dialogue come from external sources (e.g., one asks, "Does the solution solve the problem?"). In other cases the judgment comes from internal sources (e.g., one asks, "Does the person experiencing the personal dilemma being discussed feel relieved?").

Another crucial variable is the *role relationship between participants.* Again, a bipolar continuum is helpful in conceiving this dimension. On the one hand, in some dyadic interactions the roles of each person differ or are *imbalanced* (e.g., in an instructional context the teacher has knowledge that the student is seeking). On the other hand, there are instances in which the roles are relatively *equivalent* (e.g., in a marriage context to achieve intimacy, usually the two participants mutually share their perceptions and feelings).

A *comprehensive* program of interpersonal communication, one concerned with including every kind of dyadic experience, would draw from all of the following quadrants:

	Balanced	*Imbalanced*
External	problem-solving debate creative synthesis	informing or teaching interview sales pitch
Internal	personal intimacy conflict resolution (re: opinions) socializing	helping choice-making consciousness-raising

Comprehensiveness is not the only criterion for selecting dyadic experiences. If time is limited and an individualized approach to learning is valued, the personal relevance of a task to a student may be considered. Although students may be asked to undertake the entire array of dyads, some freedom of choice may be permitted on the basis of the following orientations:

1. Pragmatic approach — the student selects tasks which are used most often now (or will be used in the future), those most useful.

2. Therapeutic approach — the student selects tasks with which he or she has the most difficulty, ones which apply in relationships which he or she wants to improve.

3. Human potential approach — the student selects tasks rarely engaged in, those he or she tends to avoid or believes he or she can't do well.

4. Personal responsibility approach — the student selects tasks which he or she most wants to do, which are believed to be beneficial.

How Are Students and Tasks Matched?

Matching partners for dyadic interaction can greatly influence the value of the experience. In this format, the nature of the person with whom the interaction is shared can shape the experience as deeply as can the nature of the task being undertaken. The choice can be made upon several bases, each of which has some educational value. Several bases for matching students and an approach to employing them are outlined.

143

We know that people *attracted* to each other can exert more mutual influence than people randomly paired.[21] Consequently, one way to make the dyad a significant experience is to ask students to select partners themselves.

When people are matched who have *contrasting* ways of relating, they can each have close contact with someone who sees and responds to the world differently than they do. This adds a new perspective to their awareness. Aggressive people can learn how reserved people feel and react, and vice versa.

Matching people with *similar* approaches to communication allows for greater empathy and sharing of comparable perceptions.[22] People gain as much from learning that their way of dealing with people is not unique and feeling supported in it as they gain from learning about alternative points of view.*

Finally, students often find it valuable to be matched with classmates who share *traits similar to others* with whom they deal outside of school. This mode of pairing provides a laboratory, almost a role-playing, experience for trying new ways of relating or trying fuller honesty in feedback without the risk of damaging relationships in which they are deeply invested.

Since each of the four methods described has its own kind of value, I usually explain the alternatives and the potential usefulness of each to my students and then allow them to select partners who offer the most promise of a rewarding dyad experience.

To facilitate their choice-making each student is asked to write a self-characterization sketch, following a pattern introduced by George Kelly as part of his fixed-role therapy system.[23] Kelly asks his clients to describe themselves as they would a character in a play; writing their sketch as it might be written by a friend who knows them very intimately and sympathetically, perhaps better than anyone ever really could know them. He stresses use of the third person, to start out by saying, "John Doe is _____."

These sketches are then reproduced, and copies are distributed to all students. The four approaches to pairing are discussed as the bases upon which they are to identify the individuals with whom they might most profitably interact. The sketches are kept anonymous to minimize the influence of extraneous choice factors. Students are asked to select several more people than they actually will be matched with, so that enough pairings can be arranged which seem mutually rewarding. This system for matching dyadic partners has evoked higher satisfaction scores than any of the other approaches I have used over the years.

---

* The *contrasting* and *similar* methods of matching dyadic partners are each somewhat more appropriate for one of the types of tasks mentioned in the preceding section. Tasks in which the roles are *imbalanced* would be better suited to dyads in which the partners are *similar*, since at least one must take on a role that is atypical, thereby providing a new experience. Tasks in which the roles are *balanced* would be better suited to dyads made up of *contrasting* people, since the task prohibits them from naturally slipping into their typical, perhaps dominant or submissive roles, and again a new experience is more likely.

Under What Conditions Should Dyads Be Held?

Several issues enter into designing the conditions in which the dyadic work takes place. They include the following:

1. *Time.* Students report that the *longer* the dyad is meaningfully extended the richer a learning experience it is. Perhaps this is because the initial stages of a relationship generally are impersonal. People are sizing one another up, interacting on the basis of broad cultural and social stereotypes.[24] Only after this feeling-out phase helps each person become oriented to the other can deeper probes explore each individual and the process of their interaction be undertaken comfortably and honestly. Students usually report that dyads that end within the first hour and a half are least rewarding, those that continue for three hours or more provide the richest learning experiences.

2. *Place.* In order to go beyond what commonly is exchanged in classroom or casual campus interactions, the setting usually must be nonacademic. Students report that their apartments, a park, or a quiet tavern have been most conducive to lengthy intimate dialogue. A time period, such as the evening, with no set deadline is also recommended so that the dyad can run to its natural end without interruption.

3. *Arrangements.* Establishing the time and place for the dyad seems best done outside of class time by the two people who are to work together. By making contact and deciding when and where to meet independently, they are simulating more closely the process of reaching out to one another that must occur when people decide to pursue a relationship not mandated by course requirements. This step seems to develop a deeper sense of self-directed learning.

4. *Sequence.* Contacting and meeting with a relative stranger for a lengthy, intimate encounter is a risky step to take. Therefore, I allow students to meet with designated partners in whatever order they choose, to maximize their initial sense of safety and their chance of having a gratifying experience. At the beginning of a semester students usually feel some reluctance to try this mode of relating. Although positive experiences are the rule rather than the exception, they often expect the worst and pleasant encounters come as a surprise. Cushioning the first few tries as much as possible helps to build their faith in each other.

5. *Structuring.* The amount of structure needed to make a dyad effective varies with the topic and the students involved. Some people, dealing with some themes, need only the smallest sense of direction to proceed productively. Others will expend their entire time together in aimless small talk which they themselves later see as wasteful, unless they are given a clear plan to follow. Consequently, what has

worked best is suggesting such a plan for each dyadic session with an invitation to change or discard it should that seem worthwhile. It matters very little that a preordained structure be followed, as long as the general theme is considered, the interactions stretch the students' limits, and the process is carefully examined. In fact, the only restriction on their behavior worth enforcing is that their dialogue provide meaningful answers to the feedback questions which have been posed. (These questions are discussed in the last section of this chapter.)

How Are Learnings Drawn from Dyadic Experiences?

The dyad becomes a potent learning experience if either one or both of the following conditions are met: First, it inspires communicative behaviors that are beyond what the participants customarily would employ in their everyday lives (i.e., it expands their concept of what they can *do*). Second, it generates more *awareness* of their communication process and what affects it than each had had before (i.e., they expand the range of what is *conscious*, and hence under their control, when communicating). The dyad should be somewhat structured to maximize these ends.

The first goal can be achieved by designing exercises that force an extended, focused dialogue in an area that is usually dealt with tentatively, briefly, or not at all in casual social discourse. Several examples of "behavior-expanding" dyadic tasks follow.

1. People who wouldn't ordinarily be attracted to each other by propinquity, similarity, etc., and who would ordinarily talk very impersonally can be encouraged to share more of their personal worlds by the following dyadic exercise.

    Share with each other your personal points of view on the topics listed. This means in regard to your *own* life, not about the topic in general. You might begin by rating them according to the ease with which you feel ready to discuss them. Put an "E" next to those areas that you would find "easy" to talk about; put an "H" next to those that are "harder" to talk about; and put an "S" next to really "sensitive" areas. Then one person should pick an E area and share how it is dealt with in his or her life. The other person then offers his or her perspective. Next, the second person chooses an E topic and shares his or her view of it, after which the first person responds. Alternate this way until the E's have been exhausted and proceed as far through the H's and the S's as you wish. Neither of you should feel pressured to reveal *anything* you don't want to. Probing questions are OK, but "I'd rather not say any more about that" is always an appropriate answer, too. Of course, you should agree to keep your conversation confidential.

146

a) Your religious views and practices
b) Your political views and practices
c) Your sexual views and practices
d) Your drug use and views
e) Your entertainment preferences
f) Your past, present, and future work experiences and hopes
g) Your financial situation
h) Your relationships with family, friends, etc.
i) Your image of yourself — positive and negative factors
j) The past and present condition of your health
k) Anything else to which you react strongly

2. People who ordinarily are only comfortable when maintaining cordial, pleasant, "nice" relationships, who tend to avoid conflict, can be encouraged to experience their ability to deal with this dimension of human relations by the next dyadic exercise.

Perhaps you are paired with someone whose orientation to many issues is different from yours or from most of your friends. Take advantage of those differences by focusing on them as fully as possible. Discover on what issues you disagree and then discuss them at length. You might identify these by going through a newspaper and stopping at anything about which either of you has an opinion (i.e., a headline, an editorial, an advertisement, a cartoon, etc.). Share your opinions until you clearly understand each other, then move on. Or, you might use the following list of controversial issues as a starting point:

a) Men's and women's liberation
b) Race relations
c) Energy policies
d) America's Middle East or general foreign policies
e) Inflation
f) Environmental protection
g) Education (at a particular university)
h) Sorority, fraternity values
i) Religion

3. People who have difficulty in perceiving the impact of nonverbal messages on communication, who rely on verbal, linear, rational means of relating to reality, can be encouraged to experience how much can be perceived and exchanged without words by the following dyadic exercise.

If you get together on a pleasant spring day, you might prefer to spend the entire time without saying a word! Take a walk together through a variety of settings just looking, touching, listening, even tasting and smelling lots of varied stimuli. Walk, dance, run, crawl, sit silently together. Communicate only nonverbally. Take turns being leader on your trek; try walking while one person's eyes are closed and the other guides him or her around; observe people and animals, interact with them. See what's available when words don't get in the way. Spend your last half hour together talking over your experience.

In each of the samples offered, and in countless others (see chapter 4), the first means for stimulating communicative growth is employed: students are asked to prolong and deepen their experience with a type of discourse that they use infrequently. This enlarges their sense of what they can do with another person.

However, even if the dialogue is very ordinary, growth can still be drawn from a dyad by expanding one's *awareness* of the process. This requires making special provision for an extended, focused period of *reflection* upon the dyadic experience.

Several options exist for structuring this period of reflection. For example, it can be done by each participant *alone* or in *discussion* with the other. The following is one brief example of a dyad, requiring instructional communication, that could arise as an everyday event:

Share with each other at length who you are and what interests you are into. Then identify something in each of your lives — an activity, a skill, a person, an interest—that one would like to learn about or experience and that the other would like to share. Each should have a turn as teacher or guide and as learner or participant. You might be sharing something about your home, your area of study, your hobby, your spiritual practice, your friend, a place you enjoy, etc. From this experience you might gain insight into how someone feels upon doing for the first time what is familiar to you, how well you can make that introduction, and what activities help the person to learn. Try to be open with each other about your perceptions.

Some examination of the process can be done before, during, and immediately after the experience. *Prior* to the dyad, participants might jot down or share orally with their partners their goals and expectations for the experience. At a point in the *middle* of the dyad, they might be instructed to review what has occurred and might yet be done to make it maximally beneficial. *After* the dyad is over, many choices exist for bringing into conscious awareness the patterns which prevailed during the time they interacted. Alone, and at their leisure, or together, during the last half hour or more of their dyad, time might be given to drawing inferences about what occurred.

The *focus* of awareness can be on a variety of communication processes. Partners might review what occurred with regard to processes that apply to all situations, processes that were specific to the kind of task they were addressing, or processes accentuated by the particular pair of people interacting. Their generalizations can apply to the kind of experience they had or, more subjectively, to themselves within it. This range of possibilities is summarized in the following chart:

148

Area of Focus	Process-Related Questions	Self-Related Questions
Communication	How does communication work?	How do I communicate?
Task	How does communication work re: Task X?	How do I engage in Task X?
People	How does my partner communicate?	How do I deal with this kind of partner?

There are innumerable specific questions fitting under the main headings in this chart that would help students to see connections between comments or behaviors (i.e., transactions) of which they had been unaware. Every system and theory of interpersonal relations and every kind of communication activity makes available another perspective for examining what is actually occurring. Each points to different behaviors, even to different facets of the same behavior, as being crucial in the explanation and control of what occurs.

Nevertheless, some areas in which questions might be posed to students to encourage extended reflection and (hopefully) deeper awareness of communication within any kind of dyad are suggested:

1. The first step would be to *describe* what occurred, within themselves and between them and their partners, before, during, and after the dyad. They might answer such questions as: What did you expect you would do in this session? What did you expect your partner would do? How did you expect the activity to turn out? What actually occurred? What phases or episodes were there? What were the turning points? What differences did you feel, if any, between the first half hour and the last half hour? What were your overall impressions regarding what you actually did, what your partner did, how you handled the activity? About what aspects (positive, negative, unexpected, confusing, etc.) would you like to have more awareness?

2. Using the data and questions just raised, some of the following questions might also be considered:
   a) Expectations vs. outcomes: How did each participant see the other and the activity before the dyad began and how did this view change by the time it was over? How did what they expected affect what actually did happen?
   b) The effect of context: To what extent did the time of day and the various factors in the setting, such as noise, light, atmosphere, etc., affect your interaction? How did events that immediately preceded and that you knew would follow the dyad affect each of you?
   c) The influence process: How was the course of your interaction determined? How were decisions made? What unspoken norms applied that affected what you did and did not do?

d) The affiliation process: What was the climate of your inter-action? How did you make each other feel comfortable and uncomfortable? To what extent did each of you imply or state openly how you felt during your time together?

e) The verbal and nonverbal codes: How did each use language to clarify or obfuscate your task or personal relationship? How did your props, positions, and gestures affect your interaction?

f) The task-related strategies: How did the processes employed help or hinder the achievement of the activity undertaken? How satisfied were you with your handling of the task and to what do you attribute the results?

g) Person-related variables: How did your roles as students in a class help or hinder your involvement in the role called for in the dyad? How did the age, sex, race, personality of each partner affect his or her interaction and how he or she was seen by the other?

h) Interaction dynamics: In what ways did each person's behavior trigger a reciprocal response in the other (e.g., one person's openness about himself or herself caused the other to be unusually open, or one person's warmth, apathy, or argumen-tativeness, etc., began a sequence that built into an exchange of comments that significantly redirected the whole interaction)?

i) Transfer or learning: How does this experience compare to similar interactions you have had previously? What have you gained from engaging in this task or interacting with this person that you will apply elsewhere, etc.?

Of course, any specific concepts introduced in text material or a lecture related to the dyadic task can be the focus of a question raised for students to explore together, in written reactions afterwards, or as members of a class discussion subsequent to each round of dyads.

To enhance students' awareness of how their interaction could be interpreted differently, from another perspective, they could be asked to exchange their written reactions to the experience with their partners. If many pairs of students in a class are performing the same activity in a dyad, their papers could be exchanged among them — thereby allowing them to see how that activity could be approached and handled differently by people with another set of dynamics operating between them.

Summary

The potential for student use of dyads to experience a variety of communication activities in an active, intimate medium leading to a heightened sense of personal power and awareness is limitless. Hopefully, this chapter has developed a clearer perspective of the range of alternatives available and the methods by which their potency as learning opportunities can be maximized.

Glossary

GLOSSARY

AIKIDO (*ai*—"harmony," *ki*—"spirit" or "energy," *do*—"method" or "way"). A recently developed (1925) form of martial art that emphasizes facing situations of threat or attack from a calm, centered posture, always conscious of, but avoiding rather than retaliating, the opponent's thrust or lunge. It is learned through exercises that develop relaxation, directing one's flow of energy, and a centered, grounded stance.

BIOFEEDBACK. A global term that circumscribes a variety of methods by which a person monitors the rate or state of a physical process (such as brain waves, heartbeat, muscle tension, etc.) and uses this information to learn how to gain conscious control of that process. The monitoring is usually done with a scientific instrument (such as an electroencephalograph, electrocardiograph, electromyograph) and conscious control comes from discovering what mental images or state of mind elicit change in the desired direction and then inducing those images voluntarily.

KINESICS. The study of the physical movements used in everyday interpersonal interaction, more commonly known as "body language."

KOAN. A question or puzzling situation posed by a teacher (or "roshi") of Zen meditation to a student. To answer it, logical mental processes are useless. One must drop one's usual mode of thinking and see reality from a perspective in which Buddhist concepts prevail. An example is "What was your nature before you were born?" or "What is the sound of one hand clapping?"

SAMADHI. A state of intense, absorbed concentration that emerges from deep meditation. The mind is focused on an object and holds its attention there, to the point of dissolving any sense of distinction between the observer and the observed.

SYNECTICS. A form of creative thinking which can be practiced among a group of individuals seeking to solve problems and to invent new ideas, especially in a business setting. It makes use, especially, of analogies that help people see familiar processes in new ways. For example, one asks, "If I were *process* X, what would I be doing?" "In what other situations do comparable processes exist?" etc.

T'AI-CHI-CH'UAN. A traditional Chinese system of exercise. It incorporates a series of ritualized movements which are done slowly and with great awareness. One's body is consistently relaxed and balanced throughout. The pace is steady; the flow is smooth; one is never rigid or jerky.

References

REFERENCES

Chapter 1

[1] Examples of recent best-selling nonfiction emphasizing relaxation, sensual pleasure, peace of mind, and self-acceptance are: Harold H. Bloomfield et al., *T.M.: Discovering Inner Energy and Overcoming Stress* (New York: Delacorte Press, 1975); William H. Masters et al., *The Pleasure Bond* (Boston: Little, Brown & Co., 1975); Mildred Newman and Bernard Berkowitz, *How to Be Your Own Best Friend* (New York: Ballantine Books, 1974).

[2] Examples of recent publications emphasizing control, power and influence include: Michael Korda, *Power: How to Get It, How to Use It* (New York: Random House, 1975); Robert J. Ringer, *Winning through Intimidation* (Los Angeles: Los Angeles Publishers, 1975); Manuel J. Smith, *When I Say No, I Feel Guilty* (New York: Dial Press, 1975).

[3] Herbert Benson, *The Relaxation Response* (New York: Avon Books, 1975), p. 24.

[4] Robert E. Ornstein, *The Psychology of Consciousness* (San Francisco: W. H. Freeman, 1972).

[5] Barbara Brown, *New Mind, New Body* (New York: Harper & Row, 1974).

[6] Alan Watts, *Tao: The Watercourse Way* (New York: Pantheon Books, 1975), p. 23.

[7] *Ibid.*, p. 76.

Chapter 2

[1] This process is explained in Karen Horney, *Neurosis and Human Growth: The Struggle toward Self-Realization* (New York: W. W. Norton & Co., 1950).

[2] For a full discussion of how this question can be used see *The Spiritual Teaching of Ramana Maharshi* (Berkeley: Shambhala Publications, 1972).

[3] How self-image affects perception is discussed in Ram Dass, "Sadhana and Society," *Loka — A Journal from Naropa Institute* (Garden City: Anchor Press, 1975).

[4] The concept of materialistic relating is explored in Chogyam Trungpa, *Cutting through Spiritual Materialism*, ed. John Baker (Berkeley: Shambhala Publications, 1974).

[5] For a full discussion of this direction for personal growth see Claudio Naranjo, *The One Quest* (New York: Viking Press, 1972).

[6] The process of encountering disagreements between marital partners is described in George R. Bach and Peter Wyden, *The Intimate Enemy* (New York: William Morrow & Co., 1969).

[7] For a full discussion of how conflicts are avoided or faced see Virginia M. Satir, *Conjoint Family Therapy*, rev. ed. (Palo Alto: Science and Behavior, 1967).

[8] How one can work on oneself by examining daily life is described in Baba Ram Dass, *The Only Dance There Is* (Garden City: Anchor Press, 1974) and Chogyam Trungpa, *Meditation in Action* (Berkeley: Shambhala Publications, 1969).

[9] The role of Sabbath rest in Judaism is described in Abraham J. Heschel, *Earth Is the Lord's and the Sabbath* (New York: Harper & Row, 1978).

[10] For a full discussion of how unexpected reactions are used in psychotherapy to catalyze change, see Paul Watzlawick et al., *Change: Principles of Problem Formation and Problem Resolution* (New York: W. W. Norton & Co., 1974).

[11] Such techniques for opening up an alternate way of seeing reality are described in Carlos Castaneda, *Journey to Ixtlan* (New York: Pocket Books, 1974).

[12] The anxiety caused by a distorted sense of oneself and one's need is discussed in Peter Koestenbaum, *Managing Anxiety* (Englewood Cliffs: Prentice-Hall, 1974).

[13] Integration of these two systems for personal growth is developed in Severin Peterson, *A Catalogue of the Ways People Grow* (New York: Ballantine Books, 1971) and John Mann, ed., *Learning to Be: The Education of Human Potential* (New York: Free Press, 1972).

[14] This approach to meditation is discussed in Mahasi Sayadaw, *Practical Insight Meditation* (San Francisco: Unity Press, 1972).

[15] Reevaluation counseling is explained in Harvey Jackins, *Human Side of Human Beings: The Theory of Re-Evaluation Counseling* (Seattle: Rational Island, 1965).

[16] Progoff's theory is developed in Ira Progoff, *The Symbolic and the Real* (New York: McGraw-Hill, 1974).

[17] The use of introspective questions in communication education is discussed in Paul Friedman, "Introspection: An Approach to Individualizing Communication Instruction" (Unpublished paper presented at the 1974 convention of the Speech Communication Association, Chicago; available from author).

[18] The concept of communicating for conscious or unconscious payoffs is developed in Eric Berne, *Transactional Analysis in Psychotherapy* (New York: Ballantine Books, 1973).

[19] The effect of irrational fears on communication is explained by Albert Ellis, *Humanistic Psychotherapy: The Rational-Emotive Approach*, ed. Edward Sagarin (New York: Julian Press, 1973).

[20] The value of seeing alternatives for personal behavior is explored in Louis Raths et al., *Values and Teaching: Working with Values in the Classroom* (Columbus, Ohio: Charles E. Merrill, 1966).

[21] The use of imagination or fantasy for personal insight is developed by Herbert Otto, *Fantasy Encounter Games* (New York: Barnes & Noble, 1974).

[22] The process of role-reversal was developed by J. L. Moreno, *Who Shall Survive: Foundations of Sociometry, Group Psychotherapy, and Sociodrama* (Beacon, N.Y.: Beacon House, n.d.).

[23] The use of koans in the Rinzai School of Zen is explained in Issu Miura and Ruth F. Sasaki, *Zen Koan* (New York: Harcourt Brace Jovanovich, 1966).

[24] Looking at the historical development of one's traits is explained by Claude Steiner, *Scripts People Play* (New York: Grove Press, 1974).

[25] This process of sharing with peers is used in many self-help groups, such as Alcoholics Anonymous, Synanon, Weight Watchers, etc., e.g., Guy Endore, *Synanon* (New York: Doubleday and Co., 1968).

[26] Examples of such teaching stories are found in the works of Idries Shah, e.g., *Tales of the Dervishes* (New York: E. P. Dutton and Co., 1970) and Martin Buber, e.g., *Tales of the Hasidim*, 2 vols. (New York: Schocken Books, 1947).

[27] The process of sensory awareness is described in Charles V. Brooks, *Sensory Awareness* (New York: Viking Press, 1974).

[28] How the approach of death affects one's view of life is described in Elisabeth Kubler-Ross, ed., *Death: The Final Stage of Growth* (Englewood Cliffs: Prentice-Hall, 1975).

[29] These methods are described in Marvin Karlins and Lewis Andrews, *Biofeedback* (New York: J. B. Lippincott Co., 1972); Edmund Jacobson, *Anxiety and Tension Control: A Physiologic Approach* (New York: J. B. Lippincott Co., 1964); Al C. Huang, *Embrace Tiger, Return to Mountain: The Essence of T'ai Chi* (Moab, Utah: Real People Press, 1973).

[30] Methods are described in Swami Satchidananda, *Integral Yoga — Hatha* (New York: Holt, Rinehart, & Winston, 1970); Roberta D. Miller, *Psychic Massage* (New York: Harper & Row, 1975); Koichi Tohei, *Aikido in Daily Life* (Hackensack, N.J.: Wehman, 1974).

[31] The entire topic of consciousness-altering experiences is discussed in Andrew Weil, *The Natural Mind* (New York: Houghton Mifflin Co., 1972).

[32] Meditation that encourages mindfulness is described in Shunryu Suzuki, *Zen Mind, Beginner's Mind*, ed. Trudy Dixon (New York: John Weatherhill, 1970).

[33] The special conditions prevailing at Esalen are described by John Heider, "Chaos and Creativity at Esalen," in Bernard Aaronson, ed., *Workshops of the Mind* (New York: Doubleday & Co., 1975).

[34] These approaches are described in works such as Robert Mardment and Russell Bronstein, *Simulation Games* (Columbus, Ohio: Charles E. Merrill, 1973); Viola Spolin, *Improvisation for the Theatre* (Evanston, Ill.: Northwestern University Press, 1963).

[35] The behavior modification techniques mentioned here are explained in David L. Watson and Roland G. Tharp, *Self-Directed Behavior* (Monterey: Brooks/Cole, 1972).

[36] Reality therapy was introduced by William Glasser, *Reality Therapy* (New York: Harper & Row, 1965).

[37] The study of self-disclosure is summarized in Sidney M. Jourard, *The Transparent Self*, 2nd ed. (New York: Van Nostrand Reinhold Co., 1971).

[38] The processes of Gestalt therapy are explained in Fritz Perls, *The Gestalt Approach and Eyewitness to Therapy* (Palo Alto: Science and Behavior, 1973).

[39] An example of using screaming as a means of catharsis is described in Daniel Casriel, *A Scream Away from Happiness* (New York: Grosset & Dunlap, 1972).

[40] These techniques are described in William C. Schutz, *Here Comes Everybody: Body-Mind and Encounter Culture* (New York: Harper & Row, 1972).

[41] Lowen's approach is summarized in Alexander Lowen, *Betrayal of the Body* (New York: Macmillan, 1966).

[42] Some examples of these techniques are described in Janie Rhyne, *The Gestalt Art Experience* (Monterey: Brooks/Cole, 1973); Jack J. Leedy, ed., *Poetry Therapy* (New York: J. B. Lippincott Co., 1969), etc.

Chapter 3

[1] Mary-Jeanette Smythe, Robert Kibler, Patricia Hutchings, "A Comparison of Norm-Referenced and Criterion-Referenced Measurement with Implications for Communication Instruction," *Speech Teacher* 22 (January 1973): 1-17.

[2] An annotated bibliography of 89 studies generally debunking the objectivity of most grading systems is provided in Howard Kirschenbaum, Rodney Napier, and Sidney Simon, *Wad-Ja-Get? The Grading Game in American Education* (New York: Hart Publishing Co., 1971).

[3] The concept of experiential objectives is discussed further in Richard W. Burns, *New Approaches to Behavioral Objectives* (Dubuque, Iowa: William C. Brown Co., 1972), pp. 83-85.

[4] All the approaches described in this chapter and others less relevant to interpersonal communication are discussed in Bruce R. Joyce and Marsha Weil, *Models of Teaching* (Englewood Cliffs: Prentice-Hall, 1972).

Chapter 5

[1] Larry L. Barker, *Listening Behavior* (Englewood Cliffs: Prentice-Hall, 1971) pp. 10-12.

[2] Carl H. Weaver, *Human Listening: Processes and Behavior* (Indianapolis: Bobbs-Merrill, 1972) pp. 10-11.

[3] John Lilly and Antonietta Lilly, *The Dyadic Cyclone* (New York: Pocket Books, 1977), p. 190.

[4] Monte J. Meldman, *Diseases of Attention and Perception* (Oxford: Pergamon Press, 1970), pp. 7-8.

[5] James E. Fletcher, "A Physiological Approach to the Study of Human Information Processing" (unpublished paper presented at the 1977 annual meeting of the International Communication Association held in Berlin, Germany), p. 7.

[6] *Ibid.*, p. 5.

[7] Harry J. Jerison and R. M. Pickett, "Vigilance: The Importance of the Elicited Observing Rate," *Science* 143 (1964): 970-71.

[8] Meldman, p. 6.

[9] Wendy Wyman Kritchevsky, "Relaxation," in *Beyond Sex Roles,* ed. Alice G. Sargent (St. Paul: West Publishing Co., 1977), p. 50.

[10] *Ibid.*, p. 52.

[11] Herbert Benson, *The Relaxation Response* (New York: Avon Books, 1975), pp. 162-63.

[12] David Smith, *The East-West Exercise Book* (New York: McGraw-Hill, 1976), pp. 67-70.

[13] *Ibid.*, p. 6.

[14] Harvo Yamoka, *Meditation Gut Enlightenment* (San Francisco: Heian International Publishing Co., 1974), p. 2.

[15] *Ibid.*, p. 15.

[16] George Leonard, *The Ultimate Athlete* (New York: Avon Books, 1977), pp. 93-94.

[17] Shunryu Suzuki, *Zen Mind, Beginner's Mind,* ed. Trudy Dixon (New York: John Weatherhill, 1970), p. 26.

[18] Victor Daniels and Laurence J. Horowitz, *Being and Caring* (San Francisco: San Francisco Book Co., 1976), p. 282.

[19] Joseph Goldstein, *The Experience of Insight: A Natural Unfolding,* (Santa Cruz: Unity Press, 1976), pp. 20-23.

[20] Patricia Carrington, *Freedom in Meditation* (Garden City: Doubleday, 1977), p. 5.

[21] John B. Enright, "Awareness Training in the Mental Health Professions," *Gestalt Therapy Now*, eds. Joen Fagan and Irma Lee Shepherd (Palo Alto: Science and Behavior Books, 1970), p. 210.

[22] Carl R. Rogers, "The Necessary and Sufficient Conditions of Therapeutic Personality Change," *Journal of Consulting Psychology* 21 (1957): 95–103.

[23] Two outstanding examples are: Bernard G. Guerney, Jr. et al. *Relationship Enhancement* (San Francisco: Jossey-Bass, 1977); Gerard Egan, *You and Me* (Monterey: Brooks/Cole, 1977).

Chapter 6

For further information on classroom creativity, see:

Davis, G. A. and Scott, J. A., eds. *Training Creative Thinking*. New York: Holt, Rinehart & Winston, 1971.

Eberle, Robert F. *Scamper: Games for Imagination and Development*. Buffalo: D.O.K. Publishers, 1971.

Fabun, Don. *You and Creativity*. Beverly Hills, California: Glencoe Press, 1969.

Gordon, W. J. J. *The Metaphorical Way of Learning and Knowing*. Cambridge: Porpoise Books, 1971.

Parnes, Sidney. *Creativity: Unlocking Human Potential*. Buffalo: D.O.K. Publishers, 1972.

Torrance, Paul. *Encouraging Creativity in the Classroom*. Doubuque, Iowa: William C. Brown Co., 1970.

Chapter 7

[1] Robert B. Morton, "The Patient Training Laborataory. An Adaptation of the Instrumented Training Laboratory," in Edgar Schein and Warren G. Bennis, eds., *Personal and Organizational Change Through Group Methods* (New York: John Wiley & Sons, 1965), pp. 114-51.

[2] Lawrence Solomon and Betty Berzon, "The Self-Directed Group: A New Direction in Personal Growth Learning," in Joseph T. Hart and T. M. Tomlinson, eds., *New Directions in Client-Centered Therapy* (New York: Houghton Mifflin Co., 1970), pp. 314-47.

[3] Albert Bandura, *Principles of Behavior Modification* (New York: Holt, Rinehart & Winston, 1969).

[4] Sigmund Freud, *The Basic Writings of Sigmund Freud*, translated by A. A. Brill (New York: Modern Library, 1938).

[5] Gerald Phillips, "The Problem of Reticence," *Pennsylvania Speech Annual* (1965), pp. 22-38.

[6] Roberto Assagioli, *Psychosynthesis* (New York: Viking Press, 1971).

[7] Robert Hopper and Rita C. Naremore, *Children's Speech* (New York: Harper & Row, 1973).

[8] Eric Berne, *Transactional Analysis in Psychotherapy* (New York: Grove Press, 1961).

[9] Carl Jung, *The Practice of Psychotherapy* (New York: Pantheon Books, 1954).

[10] Andrew Salter, *Conditioned Reflex Therapy* (New York: Creative Age Press, 1949).

[11] Carl R. Rogers, *Client Centered Therapy* (Boston: Houghton Mifflin Co., 1951).

[12] George A. Kelly, *The Psychology of Personal Constructs*, Volumes 1 & 2 (New York: W. W. Norton & Co., 1955).

[13] Claudio Naranjo and Robert Ornstein, *On the Psychology of Meditation* (New York: Viking Press, 1971).

[14] Franz Alexander, *Fundamentals of Psychoanalysis* (New York: W. W. Norton & Co., 1963).

[15] E. G. Williamson, "Uses of the Counseling Interview," in E. G. Kennedy, ed., *Current Status and Future Trends in Student Personnel* (Pittsburg, Kans.: Kansas State College of Pittsburg, 1961), p. 33.

[16] Albert Ellis, *Reason and Emotion in Psychotherapy* (New York: Lyle Stuart, 1962).

[17] B. J. Biddle and E. J. Thomas, *Role Theory: Concepts and Research* (New York: John Wiley & Sons, 1966).

[18] William H. Grier and Price M. Cobbs, *Black Rage* (New York: Bantam Books, 1969).

[19] Vivian Gornick and Barbara K. Moran, eds., *Woman in Sexist Society* (New York: Basic Books, 1971).

[20] Joseph E. Shorr, *Psycho-Imagination Therapy* (New York: Stratton Intercontinental Medical Book Corp., 1972).

[21] Albert I. Rabin, ed., *Projective Techniques in Personality Assessment* (New York: Springer Publishing Co., 1968).

[22] Harry Garner, "Confrontation Problem-Solving Therapy" in Ratibor-Ray M. Jurjevich, ed., *Direct Psychotherapy: 28 American Originals*, 2 vols. (Coral Gables, Florida: University of Miami Press, 1973), pp. 328–69.

[23] Victor E. Frankl, *Man's Search for Meaning*, rev. ed. (New York: Beacon Press, 1963), p. 157.

[24] David L. Watson and Ronald G. Tharp, *Self-Directed Behavior* (Monterey: Brooks/Cole, 1972).

[25] Louis Raths, Merrill Harmin, and Sidney Simon, *Values and Teaching: Working with Values in the Classroom* (Columbus, Ohio: Charles E. Merrill, 1966).

[26] Karen Horney, *Neurosis and Human Growth* (New York: W. W. Norton & Co., 1950).

[27] Frederick S. Perls, *Gestalt Therapy Verbatim* (Moab, Utah: Real People Press, 1969).

[28] William Glasser, *Reality Therapy* (New York: Harper & Row, 1965).

[29] Teodoro Ayllon and Nathan H. Azrin, *The Token Economy: A Motivational System for Therapy and Rehabilitation* (New York: Appleton-Century-Crofts, 1968).

[30] J. L. Moreno, *Psychodrama*, Vol. 3 (Boston: Beacon House, 1969).

[31] Everett Shostrom, *Man, the Manipulator* (New York: Abingdon Press, 1967).

Chapter 8

For further information on group experiences, see:

Bunker, D. R. "Individual Application of Laboratory Training." *Journal of Applied Behavioral Science* 1 (1965): 131–48.

Campbell, J. P. and Dunnette, M. D. "Effectiveness of T-Group Training and Development." *Psychological Bulletin* 70 (1968): 73–104.

Dunnette, M.D. "People Feeling: Joy, More Joy, and the 'Slough of Despond.'" *Journal of Applied Behavioral Science* 5 (1969): 25–44.

House, R. J. "T-Group Education and Leadership Effectiveness. A review of the empiric literature and a critical evaluation." *Personnel* 20 (1967): 1–32.

Maslow, Abraham H. *Toward a Psychology of Being.* 2nd ed. New York: Van Nostrand Reinhold Co., 1968.

McConnell, H. K. "Individual Differences as Mediators of Group Behavior and Self-Perceived Change in Two Human Relations Laboratories." *Organizational Behavior and Human Performance* 6 (1971): 550–72.

Rogers, Carl R. "The Process of the Encounter Group." In *Challenges of Humanistic Psychology*, ed. James F. Bugental. New York: McGraw-Hill, 1967.

Shostrom, E. L. "Group Therapy: Let the Buyer Beware." *Psychology Today* 2 (1969): 36–40.

Schutz, William C. *Here Comes Everybody.* New York: Harper & Row, 1972.

Chapter 9

[1] The primacy of the dyad in college student communication is reported in Paul H. Fischer, "An Analysis of the Primary Group," *Sociometry* 16 (August, 1953): 272–76.

[2] Studies indicating the degree of intimacy, openness, and mutual concern common to dyads are reported by A. Paul Hare, "Size of Group as a Factor in the Interaction Profile," in *Small Groups: Studies in Social Interaction*, rev. ed., Robert F. Bales et al., eds. (New York: Alfred A. Knopf, 1965), pp. 495–512.

[3] The major role propinquity usually plays in forming friendships is described in Leon Festinger, S. Schachter and K. Back, *Social Pressures in Informal Groups: A Study of Human Factors in Housing* (New York: Harper & Row, 1959).

[4] The tendency to see people in terms of broad traits or stereotypes is described in Gustav Ichheiser, *Appearances and Realities: Misunderstanding in Human Relations* (San Francisco: Jossey-Bass, 1970).

[5] The self-awareness provided by new kinds of encounters and feedback is explored in Nena O'Neill and George O'Neill, *Shifting Gears: Finding Security in a Changing World* (New York: M. Evans, 1974).

6 The psychology of attributing causality is explored in Fritz Heider, *The Psychology of Interpersonal Relations* (New York: John Wiley & Sons, 1958).

7 The limitations on self of social roles and the opportunities afforded by new contexts are dealt with in George McCall et al., *Social Relationships* (Chicago: Aldine-Atherton, 1970).

8 The first collection of such materials is William W. Wilmot, *Dyadic Communication* (Reading, Mass.: Addison-Wesley Publishing Co., 1975).

9 The purposive nature of most communication is emphasized in Gerald R. Miller and Mark Steinberg, *Between People: A New Analysis of Interpersonal Communication* (Palo Alto: Science Research Associates, 1974).

10 I. Altman, *Social Penetration* (New York: Holt, Rinehart & Winston, 1973).

11 Bobby R. Patton and Kim Giffin, *Problem-Solving Group Interaction* (New York: Harper & Row, 1973).

12 Paul Friedman, "Creative Synthesis: An Approach to a Neglected Dimension of Small Group Behavior" (Paper presented to the Central States Speech Association, April 1975, Kansas City, Mo.).

13 Edmund Amidon and E. Hunter, *Improving Teaching: The Analysis of Classroom Verbal Interaction* (New York: Holt, Rinehart & Winston, 1966).

14 Raymond S. Ross, *Persuasion: Communication and Interpersonal Relations* (Englewood Cliffs: Prentice-Hall, 1974).

15 Alan C. Filley, *Interpersonal Conflict Resolution* (Glenview, Ill.: Scott, Foresman & Co., 1974).

16 R. R. Carkhuff, *Helping and Human Relations* (New York: Holt, Rinehart & Winston, 1969).

17 Paul Friedman et al., *Life-Shaping: A Course on Creative Personal Change* (Lawrence, Kans.: University of Kansas, 1975).

18 Charles J. Stewart and William B. Cash, Jr., *Interviewing: Principles and Practices*, new ed. (Dubuque: William C. Brown Co., 1974).

19 Gerard Egan, *Encounter: Group Processes for Interpersonal Growth* (Monterey: Brooks/Cole, 1970).

20 Louis Raths et al., *Values and Teaching: Working with Values in the Classroom* (Columbus, Ohio: Charles E. Merrill, 1966).

21 Donn Byrne, "Attitudes and Attraction," in *Advances in Experimental Social Psychology*, vol. 4, ed. Leonard Berkowitz (New York: Academic Press, 1969), pp. 35-89.

22 *Ibid.*

23 George A. Kelly, *A Theory of Personality: The Psychology of Personal Constructs* (New York: W. W. Norton & Co., 1963).

24 Cf. Altman, *Social Penetration.*